MIND ACCORDING TO VEDANTA

Swami Satprakashananda

Compiled and Edited by
Ray Ellis

Sri Ramakrishna Math
Mylapore, Madras 600 004

Published by
The President
Sri Ramakrishna Math
Mylapore, Chennai-4

© Sri Ramakrishna Math, Chennai
All rights reserved

VI-3M 2C-1-2003
ISBN 81-7120-650-6

Printed in India at
Sri Ramakrishna Math Printing Press
Mylapore, Chennai-4

PUBLISHER'S NOTE

Swami Satprakashananda began preaching Vedanta at the Vedanta Society of Providence, U.S.A. in the year 1936. Later he established the Vedanta Society of St. Louis and went on ministering to the spiritual needs of admirers of Vedanta till his passing away in 1979 at the age of 91.

Well-known for his scholarly writings on Vedanta and other related subjects, Swamiji's lectures and classes on the subjects were very instructive. The present book is a collection of such lectures, dealing with the interesting subject of MIND, according to Vedanta.

We have been able to subsidize the price of the book considerably, thanks to a generous donation from Mr. Ray Ellis, a disciple of the Swami. Our thanks are also due to Swami Chetanananda, the present leader of the Vedanta Society of St. Louis, U.S.A., for kindly giving us the necessary permission to publish this book.

We hope this book will be a useful addition to the growing literature on the enigmatic subject of the human mind.

2.2.94   Publisher

PREFACE

Swami Satprakashananda was born in Dhaka, Bengal, in 1888. At the age of 12 he saw Swami Vivekananda when that great exponent of Vedanta visited Dhaka. He received a degree from Calcutta University, and then, several years later, became a monk of the Ramakrishna Order. He was assistant editor of *Prabuddha Bharata*, a magazine of the Order, for three years. He was in charge of the Ramakrishna Mission Centre in New Delhi for six years. In 1936, he was sent to the United States to conduct the work of the Vedanta Society of Providence while Swami Akhilananda was in India for the completion and dedication of the new Sri Ramakrishna Temple at the headquarters in Belur, Calcutta.

In 1938, with about three hundred dollars and the name of one person who might be of some help, he went to St. Louis and established the Vedanta Society of St. Louis. He remained there 41 years, returning to India only once in 1955. He passed away in 1979 at the age of 91. Since then the work has been carried on by another Swami of the Order.

Each chapter of this book is a lecture never before published. The lectures were delivered in the late 1950s and the 1960s, except for the chapter entitled "Psychiatry and Vedanta". This is a lecture given at a Psychotherapeutic Round Table held on 10 March, 1966, at the Central State Hospital, Louisville, Kentucky. The Swami was moderator. This lecture also appeared in the September 1966 issue of *Prabuddha Bharata*.

Swami Satprakashananda was also the author of numerous books and pamphlets; chief among them is a powerful epistemological text entitled *Methods of Knowledge According to Advaita Vedanta*. His other books include *The Goal And The Way; The Universe, God And God-realization; Meditation, its Process, Practice and Culmination; Hinduism and Christianity; Sri Ramakrishna's Life and Message in the Present Age; Swami Vivekananda's Contribution to The Present Age*, and pamphlets, "Ethics and Religion," "The Use of Symbols In Religion", and "World Peace—How?"

Special thanks are due Virginia H. Ward who tape recorded the lectures in this book and transcribed them to paper many years ago. Without the recordings this book could not have come into being.

We hope this volume will promote the understanding of that which must be understood and controlled before spiritual progress can be made—the mind. ❏

Editor

CONTENTS

		Page
	Publisher's Note	iii
	Preface	v
1.	Mind, According to Vedanta	1
2.	How to Purify the Mind	25
3.	The Mind and the Soul	46
4.	The Mind and its Ways	61
5.	The Mind and the Senses	82
6.	The Mind and its Control	98
7.	Waking, Dreaming and Deep Sleep	113
8.	Samadhi or Superconscious Experience	131
9.	Meditation: Its Purpose and Practice	151
10.	Psychiatry and Vedanta	171

1. MIND, ACCORDING TO VEDANTA

The nature of the mind is very difficult to understand, because the mind is very subtle as well as hidden. The reason so many want to know about the mind is that they find many of their problems arise from a mental condition. Even physical problems arise from mental conditions, and so the medical doctors and psychiatrists are kept busy. But you cannot have a sound mind simply by paying attention to the mind when you have mental trouble, just as you cannot expect to have good physical health if you take care of the body only when you have physical ailments.

If you want to have a good body, a healthy, strong body, you must take care of it at all times. If you depend simply on doctors and medicines, you cannot expect to have a good physical body. What are the conditions for sound physical health? You should eat wholesome food in moderate quantities and at regular hours. You should live in a congenial atmosphere, and take regular exercise. Similarly, for the development of the mind, these three courses have to be followed—wholesome food, congenial atmosphere and regular exercise. My teacher, Swami Brahmananda, used to say: "You have to feed the mind with rich food, nourish it regularly, strengthen it, enrich it. Just as, if you feed a cow well, you can get abundant rich milk; similarly, if you feed this mind well, then only can you get rich food out of it. That is, you can have peace, you can have wisdom, you can have strength, you can have joy."

Vedanta stresses, particularly, the development of the mind, because life's development means the development of the mind. Our physical development, our intellectual development, our aesthetic development, our moral development, are not possible without the cultivation of the mind. A great Hindu saint says regretfully: "The richest soil, the soil of the human mind, lies fallow. If it could be tilled well it would yield golden crops, but since it lies fallow, it yields brambles and thorny bushes and weeds." Mind is the source of freedom and also of bondage. It is a common saying in Vedanta that our joy and suffering, wisdom and folly, strength and weakness, depend very much on the condition of the mind.

Mind, according to Vedanta, is something distinct from the physical body on the one hand, and the spiritual Self on the other. It is not identified with the spiritual Self. Why? Because the spiritual Self is the knower; the mind is not the knower. Mind is an object of knowledge. Just as you perceive an external object, similarly, you can observe your own mind. Since it is an object of knowledge, an object of cognition, mind cannot be the knower. You are essentially the knower. Here is an object, a chair for instance. Do the eyes see this chair?—and do the ears hear a voice? If the ears hear and the eyes see and nose smells, what happens? You have so many knowers, so many selves in one individual. But beyond these senses there is one common knower. That knower perceives through the eyes, perceives through the ears, perceives through the nose. That knower not only is distinct from all these organs of perception, but is also distinct from the mind because that knower visualizes the mind, observes the mind. You can observe your mind directly through introspection; others can observe your mind only indirectly. Only your own mind is observable by you directly through introspection. All other methods of studying the mind are indirect.

Because the mind is an object of knowledge, consciousness is not intrinsic in the mind. Consciousness is intrinsic in the knower. The knower is self-aware, self-evident; you never question your own existence. You take it for granted that you exist: this is self-revealing—That you are. Why is the knower self-revealing? Because it is self-intelligent: self-awareness is its very essential characteristic. Such is the Self. And what is the mind? The mind is an object of knowledge, just as the chair is the object of knowledge. Naturally, mind is devoid of consciousness. Any object of knowledge is devoid of consciousness. This real Self, the knower, *per se*, is the sole self-intelligent principle in the human personality. So, according to Vedanta, mind is dark, material, just as any external object such as a clod of earth is dark and material and devoid of consciousness. Similarly, the mind is also material.

The Western distinction between mind and matter does not hold in Vedanta. Only spirit, self-luminous, is the intelligent principle. Only one principle, pure spirit, is spiritual reality—everything else is material. This is a vital difference between Vedantic thought and Western thought that should be noted. For many centuries, particularly from the time of Descartes, for nearly three hundred years, there has been this differentiation in Western thought, this dualism between mind and matter. Why this difference? Because it has been the practice to identify the mind, or to unite the mind, with the real Self, the pure spirit. Thus, mind is distinguished from matter. This practice has prevailed during the past centuries in the West. At the present time there is another tendency, quite opposite. This is the tendency to identify the mind more and more with the body.

Mind is just a function of the body, or some kind of bodily condition. The modern tendency is to unite the mind with the body, or, align the body with the mind; and the tendency for the past centuries has been to unite the mind with the Self. Naturally, mind has been distinguished from matter. But in religious thought we have noticed that in the West this distinction between the mind, the body and the Self has been maintained. In a verse from the Epistle of St. Paul to the Thessalonians (the first set of epistles, verse 23 in the fifth chapter) St. Paul says: "And the very God of peace sanctify you wholly; and I pray God your whole spirit and soul and body be preserved blameless unto the coming of our Lord Jesus Christ."

Three words are used in the above passage—*spirit, soul,* and *body*. You may say that spirit and soul are identical, that two distinct entities are not actually meant. But, if we turn to the Greek original, we find three words—soul, psyche, and mind. These words are related as soul and the body, psyche and the mind, and pneuma and pure spirit, the Self, the knower. So religion has maintained the distinction between the mind and pure spirit, but in psychological and philosophical thinking we find no difference between mind and spirit has been maintained.

In Vedanta the mind is called *antahkarana*, that is, "internal instrument." We have external instruments of cognition or perception: the eyes, the ears, the nose, the organ of taste, the organ of touch. Then there is one internal instrument called *mind*. But why recognize another internal instrument? Are not the five organs of perception just named adequate? No! You see and hear someone speak, yet if your mind moves away so that you cease to pay attention to the speaker, you won't see or hear him. You are there with a perfectly good pair of eyes and ears, but if your mind turns elsewhere you won't see or hear him.

MIND, ACCORDING TO VEDANTA

There is another variable factor, which has moved away in this case. The Self is here. If only the Self and the organ of vision were solely responsible for this visible and audible perception, then you would have seen and heard the speaker at all times. And if these were not adequate for perception, at no time would you have been able to see and hear. But, since you have perception sometimes, and you do not have perception at other times, that shows there is a third factor involved. Therefore, in each act of perception, there is an external object, there is an organ of perception (eyes, ears, etc.), there is one perceiver, the knowing Self, and there is the mind.

This mind is distinct from the Self, distinct from these organs of vision, distinct from the entire body. These are connected very closely, inseparable, but still distinct. That means mind is not an integral part of the body, nor is it an integral part of the spiritual Self—they are connected but yet are distinct. Mind is the seat of internal perception. Just as you perceive the external objects, the chair, or this wall, or the flower, or the picture, similarly, you can also perceive the internal facts. You can watch within to see if you like something or not. You can perceive your likes and dislikes, hopes and fears, joys and sorrows. And just as external perception is a criterion of existence, similarly, this internal perception is also a criterion of existence. Just as a chair or a table is real to you, so, also, your likes and dislikes, hopes and fears, your love and hatred, your joys and sorrows are real to you. These should not be identified with their physical expressions.

Love, for instance, is a fact because it is true to your inner experience. Without having any love, you can show love. You can kiss a person, speak sweet words to a person, embrace him, dance even at his very sight—a show of love—but still there may not be any love. Since these inner facts are something distinct from their physical expressions, we must acknowledge there are such realities and these realities are observable through the mind. This is also one of the reasons why you should acknowledge mind as distinct from the physical body. You react in a certain way to external objects but, even then, your mind may intervene. For instance, some food is brought to you, food that you like very much, but your mind thinks: "I like this food very much, still, it is not good for me, it is very pleasant, but not good." So you reject it. The eyes saw the food but some other power made the judgment to reject it.

Vedanta recognizes these different functions of the mind, such as cognition, feeling, willing, as the primary functions of the mind. Then there are other functions of the mind such as memory, imagination, love, hatred, hope, fear. All these belong to the mind. At the same time Vedanta considers the cognitive aspect of the mind to be primary because feeling and willing both depend on the cognitive side of the mind, because mind has the power of consciousness. Although it is devoid of consciousness, the mind, nevertheless, has the power of consciousness. The mind, being associated with the spiritual Self, gets the light of the Self, the reflected light. Mind, though it is material like any external object, is composed of very fine, rarefied matter. Because of this, mind endures, even after this body is separated. It belongs to a different order of matter than the external objects, and it has the special power to be illuminated by consciousness, so that this body is more or less illuminated by consciousness. This is why the eyes seem to perceive, the hands to touch. When you sleep the eyes cannot see, the hands cannot grasp, because consciousness almost completely recedes from the physical system. Just a little bit is left, through which the automatic activities are possible.

Mind receives the light of consciousness and, because of that, seems to have the power of feeling. Actually, it is the Self that feels through the mind. The light of the Self is reflected on the mind. Just as a piece of wire that has been permeated with fire looks radiant—and that heat can burn one's fingers—it is not the wire that burns, it is the heat energy in the wire. Similarly, it is actually not the mind that feels, that imagines, or wills, or hopes, or fears; it is the light of consciousness that enables the mind to behave this way. So, through the light of consciousness, mind has these powers and, of these powers, the power of cognition is primary, because all other powers depend on this. Unless there is some kind of cognition, or consciousness, there cannot be any feeling or willing. Feeling and willing always presuppose some measure of consciousness. For that reason Vedanta has particularly analyzed this cognitive aspect of the mind and takes into account its four states or functions: deliberation (*manas*), determination (*buddhi*), egoism (*ahamkara*), and recollection (*citta*). In every external perception these four are involved. On seeing a chair a person does not at once determine it as a chair. In the beginning he is vaguely aware of it as something. He is in an indecisive state. So he cogitates "What is it? What is it?" This function of deliberation is *manas*. Then he searches within and recalls some past impression akin to it. With this recollection he cognizes the object as "this is a chair." This function of determination is *buddhi*. The function of recollection is *citta*. With the knowledge "this a chair" arises the knowledge "I know the chair". This function of egoism is *ahamkara*. Because of the rapid succession of the four functions they seem to be instantaneous. The four functions represent four different states of the mind.

Vedanta studies the mind, particularly, as the seat of impressions. These impressions are left on the mind, not only by the perceptions of objects, but also through our activities. We have five organs of perception: the organ of hearing, the organ of seeing, the organ of taste, the organ of smell, the organ of touch. We have also five organs of action: the organ of speech, the hands, the legs, the organ of procreation, the organ of evacuation. Just as the functions of the organs of cognition leave some impression on the mind, so also the organs of action. These impressions become the source of our memory, as well as the source for our likes and dislikes.

Just as the perceptions through these cognitive organs leave impressions on the mind, similarly, the experiences through the organs of action leave impressions on the mind. You see something, some impression is left on the mind, and from that impression you can create an image of the thing. Similarly, if you speak with your organ of speech, or you hold something, or you give something, work with the hands, or move with the legs, any function that is done by these organs of action leaves an indelible impression on the mind. We generally think that only the visual perception or the auditory perception leaves an impression upon the mind. This is not so. Actions, also, leave impressions upon the mind; and these impressions create tendencies within you, create your disposition within you, create a tendency to work in the same way again. These impressions live within us.

Our experiences and our activities are constantly leaving impressions upon the mind. The mind is a very big storehouse for all these impressions. Not a single impression is eliminated; they are all stored there. You cannot forget even what you did in your early life when you had developed some consciousness. Some time or other, through right association, the impressions will come to the upper part of the mind. These impressions create your disposition, your tendencies, and become the source of your memory, your likes and dislikes. These impressions live within you as subtle forces that fructify as the effects of these impressions. That is, they will create for you favourable or unfavourable results. It is because of these impressions as subtle forces that we reap the fruits of our actions, sooner or later.

Vedanta very much emphasizes the fact that the mind stores impressions. These impressions lie within us, broadly speaking, in two different forms. Sometimes they are manifest, sometimes they are not. Vedanta does not divide the mind into two cut and dried compartments, or sections, as "conscious" and "unconscious". What is unconscious now can be conscious tomorrow, or an hour later even. So there is no division within the mind such as "conscious" and "unconscious".

Those impressions that are unmanifest are actually in the subconscious level. Those impressions that become manifest are within the conscious level. What is the conscious level? The conscious level is the range within the ego-consciousness. That which comes within the view of this ego-consciousness is the conscious mind. That which is outside the range, or below the range of this ego-consciousness, is the subconscious or unconscious mind. By extending the range of this ego-consciousness, what is in the "unconscious" can be brought to light.

According to Vedanta there is also the "superconscious" state. What we generally call "unconscious" is below this ego-consciousness. What we call "conscious" is within the range of this ego-consciousness. Then there is the "superconscious" state, which is beyond the range of ego-consciousness. When there is actual spiritual experience, when you realize God, then you go beyond the range of this ego-consciousness. You get out of the barriers of the ego. But, ordinarily, you are within the range of this ego-consciousness, and you have a good deal of your impressions below the range of ego-consciousness.

These unmanifest impressions lie in the subconscious mind below the ego-consciousness in three different forms. One is the *overpowered form*, another is the *attenuated form* and the third is the *dormant form*. Many of our impressions lie

MIND, ACCORDING TO VEDANTA 15

overpowered under the stress of circumstances. A person may have some wrong tendencies. Then he changes his associations, and because of the change, these wrong tendencies do not assert themselves—but they are quite strong, being overpowered only. They do not assert themselves. Similarly, if some calamity befalls us, if we lose wealth or friends, some of the wrong tendencies become overpowered for the time being. This is the state of being overpowered. This is not a very safe state. If there are dark forces within a person, and they lie overpowered because of circumstances, they can assert themselves any time. If you want a safe state, you have to gradually weaken them, attenuate them, and that is the purpose of culture, of education, of good associations. Dark forces within the mind should be attenuated gradually; they should not be simply suppressed or overpowered. They should be weakened by cultivating different tendencies, by elevating the mind. If they are overpowered only, the moment they assert themselves they will throw you overboard, in spite of the remonstrances of your reason and the resistance of your will.

There are many impressions and tendencies lying dormant in the mind, asleep. As long as they are asleep they cannot do any harm. In spite of them you can make spiritual progress, intellectual progress, moral progress. If our "unconscious" with all that is latent in it, was constantly opposing us, we would not be able to make any progress. No mind is perfect, completely free from weaknesses. Sometimes you feel angelic, and sometimes you feel just the opposite. In spite of that, intellectual, moral, and spiritual progress is possible, because as long as the impressions are dormant, they cannot resist your progress.

The "unconscious" does not only contain what we call the dark forces. Many spiritual and moral possibilities lie hidden within you in the "unconscious". Who knows what experiences you have had through your past existences. Who knows what actions you have performed in your past existences. This storehouse of impressions contains both good and bad elements.

Vedanta stresses the cultivation, the development, of the conscious mind. It is through the conscious mind that you have to overcome the "unconscious". You should not be at the mercy of the "unconscious", living in constant dread of it. You have nothing to fear from the "unconscious" because the "unconscious" works mechanically. It influences you automatically, mechanically, but the conscious mind has self-determination. With will-power you can resist. Vedanta stresses self-determination, which is the special power of the conscious mind. It is through the conscious mind that you can overcome the "unconscious". If there are wrong tendencies lying within, they have to be weakened by constant effort. It will not help very much to take care of the mind or to pay attention to the mind only at the time of difficulty. If you take care of the body only when it has an ailment, you cannot expect to have good health. You must take care of it at all times, living with good associations, eating good food, and taking regular exercise.

Normally, this rich soil of the human mind lies fallow. This is the richest soil, which, properly cultivated, can yield golden crops. If it is not cultivated, thorny bushes and weeds will grow and cause immense trouble to you. Vedanta has divided mental impressions into two distinct sections: manifest and unmanifest; however, these are not clear-cut divisions, because what is unmanifest can be manifest and what is manifest can be un-manifest.

Vedanta suggests practices for the development of the mind. Simply critical analysis of your mental condition will not help you very much. What is the process of development? One process is self-discipline. Some shudder at the idea of self-discipline. They understand it to be restraint of self-expression. In reality it is that you struggle to be at your best, to reach for the highest. If you watch your life carefully, you cannot be quite satisfied with it. There is always some kind of self-criticism within because you have a standard you can never quite live up to. There is a rift between your power of judgment and your actual living, between your rational life and your emotional life. Self-discipline is the alignment of your emotional life with your rational life, the directing of all your energies to the realization of the ideal. Whatever understanding of the ideal you have, exercise it to the fullest. Whatever other powers you have, exercise them to the fullest and see whether you can live just as you think you should. In this way you direct your life to the ideal that you conceive in your mind. Try to direct your thinking from the lower to the higher values. This is not suppressing something, you are simply changing your actions to those which you recognize as right. That is self-discipline.

Actually, you are trying to be true to yourself; you are not restraining yourself. There are inimical forces entrenched on your own ground. You succumb to them and think at the same time they are your best allies; but your best friend is your real Self. Try to be true to your own Self and give right direction to your life. Direct your life to higher and higher values. When you do that, your mind will recede from the lower values naturally. There is no question of suppression here, or repression. This self-discipline purifies the mind. It is a positive method. You have an ideal that you recognize to be right, and you try to follow that ideal. This is a direct, positive method.

Vedanta suggests another course of development called *meditation*. What should we meditate on? You can meditate on anything, but Vedanta says to meditate particularly on your real Self, your spiritual Self. Your spiritual Self is not a part of this physical body. Your spiritual Self belongs to Supreme Spirit, whom you call God, who answers all your visions of perfection. You meditate on this spiritual Self and the relation of this spiritual Self with the Divine Being.

This meditation will immediately heighten your self-consciousness.

You think you are a mortal being, subject to birth, growth, decay and death, that your power is limited, that you are weak and impure. You align yourself constantly with this physical body, and through the physical body with all that is concerned with this physical body. So, naturally, although you are essentially immortal, pure, free and luminous, you think you are dark, you have old age, decay and death, birth, hunger, thirst, heat, cold—so many things hampering you. But if you meditate on your spiritual Self, at once your self-consciousness will be expanded. As soon as this consciousness of pure Spirit dawns on the horizon of the mind, your faith is strengthened because that is the source of your faith and your strength. By thus meditating you become pure, stronger, wiser, happier.

As you meditate on this spiritual Self, you develop better power of introspection. You come to know your mind much better, and, if you know your mind, it cannot play tricks on you. Deceitfulness of the mind comes about because, to a large extent, the mind escapes our notice and our cognition. The more you know the mind, the less will be the trickery of the mind.

This practice of meditation develops your power of introspection. You can clearly see the workings of the mind, and, also, your range of vision is extended. You see the impressions that seemed to be unconscious are actually thwarting your progress. These are the impressions that pull you about in directions you didn't intend to go. So you become self-aware, and this self-awareness is the very secret of control of the mind and the body. You fail to control the body and the mind because you identify yourself with them, you are submerged in the waves of the mind. When you distinguish yourself from this body, from this mind, from this psychophysical system as a whole, and know that you are pure Spirit, you at once gain the power to dominate this psychophysical system. Through the practice of meditation on the spiritual Self, you gradually develop power over the psychophysical system. Whatever else you do, as long as you do not know your fundamental position in this psychophysical system, as long as you identify yourself with, and are lost in the waves of the mind and the waves of the body, there is no secret by which you can actually control the body and the mind.

If you want to stand on your own two legs, practise meditation to develop your true self-awareness and try to objectify this entire psychophysical system and bring it under control. This power of meditation is the source of your knowledge and the source of your strength, because, if you want to know anything, you must know it through concentration of the mind. Tremendous energy is frittered away through lack of concentration. My teacher (Swami Brahmananda) used to say: "If you lose a little money, or a bit of time for the sake of another person, you regret it; but how much mental energy you are wasting every moment simply because you have not the power to fasten the mind to the particular object to which you want it to be fastened, or, because you cannot detach the mind from what you want to detach it. You are losing energy constantly because of this."

The practice of meditation develops the power of concentration, which is the great source of knowledge. Whatever knowledge you acquire, you acquire through the practice of concentration. The more the power of concentration, the greater is the power of acquiring knowledge, and concentration also means the conservation of energy.

MIND, ACCORDING TO VEDANTA

This practice of concentration gives you not only the power of concentrating on a particular subject, it also gives the power of detachment. These two powers, the power of attachment and the power of detachment, must go together. Everybody, sometime or other, becomes concentrated on something, but that concentration is not within your power. The mind moves at its own sweet will. It becomes fastened on something and you cannot get it unfastened. Worries and reveries come and we watch them and succumb to them helplessly. A certain thing has been done by me, and my mind ponders over that again and again. I cannot detach the mind. The power of detachment is very necessary as is the power of attachment. Through the practice of concentration of the mind these important powers of attachment and detachment are developed.

Vedanta has analyzed the human mind and has assigned its exact place in the human personality. At the same time Vedanta has prescribed courses for the development of the mind. Prevention is much better than cure. Only curative methods will not do. Preventive methods have to be adopted.

When this is done, control over the mind is won. ◻

2. HOW TO PURIFY THE MIND

The importance of the human mind cannot be overestimated. Man's progress—material, intellectual, aesthetic, moral, and spiritual—depends on the development of the mind. There is no development, actually, in man's spiritual Self. Spiritual development means the development of the mind so that the self-luminous, pure, free spirit can find more and more expression.

Sunlight may appear to us through different mediums, and the manifestation of the light depends on the nature of the medium. Similarly, in one's spiritual life, there is no development of the self-luminous, pure, immortal, ever free spirit. There is only mental development that reveals to the seeker a greater or lesser degree of the spiritual light.

The mind is said to be one's greatest friend as well as one's worst enemy. If the mind is fully controlled, then it will prove to be your best friend; but if you lose control over the mind; it will prove to be your worst enemy. Our strength and weakness, happiness and unhappiness, knowledge and ignorance, freedom and bondage, all depend on the nature or condition of the mind. And, unless the mind is sound, we cannot have even sound physical health.

The greatest obstacles to the mind's development are the impurities of the mind. These impurities do not actually inhere in the mind, but they adhere to the mind. No sin actually forms an intrinsic part of the mind. Just as dust may adhere to a crystal, similarly, mind, which is intrinsically as pure as a crystal has impurities or sins, or whatever you may call them, adhering to it. They are not inherent in the mind. The human mind, however restless it may appear to be, however impure it may appear to be, is essentially made of the purest material stuff.

Vedanta differentiates between the mind and the real Self. The real Self has no change. It is pure spirit; that is what a man really is, but he has a mind through which this Self is manifested. The mind is the finest of all the material substances, and it is pure. Because of that, the mind has the capacity to manifest knowledge; that is, the mind has the capacity to radiate consciousness. It has that special capacity because it is made of pure substance. So, actually, there is no impurity or sin in the mind, not to speak of the spiritual Self, which is ever pure and free. But even the mind is basically pure.

All the impurities you try to get rid of adhere to the mind, and these impurities cause restlessness of the mind. Calmness of mind is not possible when there are impurities in the mind. These impurities are the obstacles to the mind's development. Unless the mind is calm, one cannot concentrate the mind on anything. A scientist, a philosopher, a businessman, a political leader, has to concentrate his mind on the object of study to gain the required knowledge. Unless the mind is pure to a certain extent at least, the mind cannot be calm. And unless the mind is calm, you cannot concentrate the mind on any subject and you cannot gain any knowledge. It is through the mind that you know whatever you know.

You do not see things just through the eyes. If you are absent-minded, as the saying goes, you cannot see things. Your ears may be open, but still you will not hear if your mind is somewhere else. It is not just the ears that hear, the eyes that see, even the hands cannot work if your mind does not join with the hands. Can you cook a good dinner if your thoughts are elsewhere? It is because the mind is associated with the body and the organs that the body and the organs can function correctly, and the sense organs can know things correctly.

Whatever we know from the grossest sense object to the highest spirituality, we know through the mind. Whenever we know anything there is a corresponding modification of the mind. That is, there is a modification in the mind corresponding to the object of knowledge. And the more the mind corresponds to the object of knowledge, the greater or more accurate is the knowledge. Any secular knowledge you have, you gained through the concentration of the mind; this concentration cannot be achieved unless the mind is calm. Calmness of mind is not possible unless the mind is pure. Not to speak of secular knowledge, spiritual knowledge is impossible to attain except through the full concentration of the mind. Through deep meditation your mind becomes completely absorbed in God, tranquil and transparent, and suffused with the light of divinity. Only then is direct perception of divinity possible. This is the state of samadhi. So you see the importance of the puri-

HOW TO PURIFY THE MIND

fication of the mind. You must attain calmness and concentration of the mind, only then can you know whatever it is you want to know.

Now what are these impurities adhering to the mind? Impurities exist in us in many gross and subtle forms. They exist on the surface of the mind and they also exist in the bottom of the mind. Patanjali says that there are five kinds of impurities: the basic impurity of the mind is (1) ignorance. You do not know the truth, and you are always interested in untruth. You do not know the real, and you are interested in the unreal. You do not know the eternal and you are interested in the temporal. This is basic ignorance. In addition, you do not know your true nature, you do not know your relationship with the Supreme Being, and you have (2) egoism—identification of the real Self with the not-self. You identify yourself with the psychophysical system, which is not the real you. This is egoism. Being identified with the psychophysical system, you become identified more or less with this physical universe. This mistaken identification brings on (3) attachment, (4) aversion, and (5) infatuation with the world. According to Patanjali, these are the different impurities that adhere to the mind.

From our common experiences we can see that the impurities that dwell in the human mind mostly are the gross emotions, generally called passions. Lust, greed, anger, jealousy, hatred: these are the grossest impurities. They upset the mind at once. They distort our judgement, our vision is blurred, we cannot see things rightly. In order to get rid of this distortion, Patanjali has suggested that we think of their harmfulness—how they upset the mind and rob it of all peacefulness. We cannot have right understanding, we cannot have peace of mind, we cannot have happiness, we cannot have even strength of mind if we indulge in all these things.

A person should think over the harmfulness of the wrong emotions and try to get rid of them. If one can be convinced of their harmfulness, that will be the first step toward the conquering of these emotions. And then one should cultivate the virtues that are their opposites: for example, one should try to overcome pride by the cultivation of humility. One should also try to conquer avarice by considering the harmfulness of avarice, and then by using discretion as to how the object can be gained by exercising the power one has. If one desires things that are

HOW TO PURIFY THE MIND 31

quite impossible, naturally one will be frustrated. By right judgement one can exercise the virtues to try and overcome the undesirable passions.

Then there are also evil thoughts. Even when the passions do not prevail within, you may still think of them. You may not steal somebody's property, still you may think of stealing it. You may not have all the passions within you, still thoughts about them may come within your mind. These thoughts have to be conquered by feeding the mind with noble thoughts. Our teacher used to ask us to study the lives of the great ones, read their messages and draw inspiration from them. If you feed the mind with rich and healthy food, then the mind will gain noble thoughts, strength, knowledge, peace, and so forth. Never lose the opportunity of feeding the mind with proper, wholesome food.

There are other impurities that cloud the mind such as prejudices, misconceptions, doubts, superstitions—these should all be overcome by cultivating right knowledge. Use your power of discrimination as far as possible to see things from the right viewpoint, to understand things. Do not state your opinion concerning something you know nothing about. It is a very common occurrence to assert ignorance as authority. A person will pass judgment on religion, or on God, or on this or that person, and if you analyse the source of this person's knowledge, you find ignorance is the only source of authority. We should have correct understanding and knowledge of things to get rid of misconceptions.

Doubts are also impurities, as well as cares and worries and fears. These often depend more on our imagination than on the actual reading of the situation. When this mind is assailed with fears, we should see how far these fears are real, and how far imaginary. If we analyse those fears we will see that they are not so much, and that whatever fears there are, there is a solution to them. Know that there is no plight in this life from which there is no escape, and there is no problem that cannot be solved. We should always read the situation very carefully, with a balanced mind, and find the best way out of the difficulty.

Even when these obstacles or impurities do not prevail in the conscious mind, still they live within us in our subconscious mind as subtle forces. They may manifest themselves in the conscious mind any time. Our weaknesses lie very

HOW TO PURIFY THE MIND

much hidden within the mind as they do not always prevail in the conscious mind. These subtle forces are called *samskaras*, impressions. They live within us in three forms: the latent form, overpowered form, and in attenuated form.

These impressions come from our experiences in life. We experience various things in this world, and each thing experienced through any of the sense organs leaves an indelible impression on our mind. Our memories come out of these impressions. Our tendencies and our desires are manufactured from these impressions. The more concerned we are with something, the deeper is the impression. The cause of these concerns is attachment or aversion. We are concerned if something is very disagreeable to us. If the thing is just a trifle to us we overlook it. So behind these interests, which are the cause of our impressions, there is both attachment and aversion. Therefore, we should be very careful in gathering impressions.

If we see wrong pictures, hear wrong sounds, meet wrong kinds of persons, then wrong impressions will be constantly collecting within us. These impressions will be stored up and will manifest themselves again in the future. We cannot blame others for this. Vedanta says,

"Your hands hold the rope that binds you." We are creating our own impressions, our attachments and aversions by our own actions in life. We store these impressions and become victims of them when they become manifest in the conscious mind. We must be careful in this life, and try to gather good and wholesome impressions that will uplift us. In exercising the five sense organs, we should be careful to gather right impressions as much as possible.

Our works also create impressions. If we treat people with the object of helping, with a charitable disposition, it will create a charitable disposition within us. If we do anything with anger, with spite, it will create an impression of spitefulness. In this way, by our actions, we are developing our inner nature. Actions, being repeated, produce repeated impressions in the mind, and these repeated impressions become manifest as disposition. So we must be very discretionary in our actions. Everything pleasant is not good: this is a tragic element in life. So we must exercise our judgement. "Yes, it appears pleasant. I am emotionally drawn to this, but it is not wholesome." We must exercise discretion in this life: we must control our actions, control our experiences, gather wholesome impressions

HOW TO PURIFY THE MIND 35

within as much as possible. These wholesome impressions will create our memories, our thoughts, our disposition, our desires and tendencies. These will manifest themselves within our mind.

Behind these impressions are desires, interest in the sense objects. Our interests in this world naturally attract us, because we are created with outward tendencies. We seek these objects because we don't know anything higher than sense pleasures in various forms. But these sense pleasures, or sense objects, do not count as much as our moral virtues. Moral values are higher than, and superior to, material values. We may amass wealth, but if we do not have virtues within us, we will never have the right understanding to utilize wealth to our own advantage. We may gain intellectual power, scientific power, or some other power, but we will not have the right understanding to utilize that power. That understanding comes through the purification of the mind, through the practice of virtue. It is virtue that brightens the intellect. It is virtue that develops insight within.

Apparently, material possessions are very grand and attractive and valuable, but your inner life is much more important. A single weakness like jealousy can make a person miserable for life. Think of that. Just an element of suspicion can ruin your life. An element of attachment can break a family. Wealth in many forms, pleasures, luxuries, and superfluities do not count as much as moral strength. As long as you consider material objects or material values as the primary objectives of life, you cannot practise virtue in the true sense, because whenever there is a clash between a material objective and your observing some moral principle, you will adhere to the material objectives rather than to moral principle. But Vedanta declares unequivocally that material objects do not help you as much as moral virtues. You can't practise virtue as a principle, unless you consider virtue as a value in itself, a value superior to material possessions.

We talk highly of justice and peace in the world, but our mind is always looking for material power, glory, and acquisition. As soon as there is a clash between our material interest and our understanding of justice, we give up justice. We hold to the material interest by all means possible. This is what happens in the world in collective life as well as in individual life.

HOW TO PURIFY THE MIND 37

It is to be understood that if you really want to practise virtue in the true sense, if from virtue you want to acquire strength and peace and freedom, then you should know that virtue is a value in itself and superior in importance to material possessions. For the sake of virtue you may give up material interest, but you should never give up virtue for material interests. You will be the loser. It will defeat your purpose. If you can hold to this principle, then you have come to the first landmark of mental purification. You must be convinced of this idea: virtue is a path in itself, principle is strengthening. If you give up principle it will weaken you. When you are convinced of this, you can consistently follow the moral path, the ethical ideal, in the true sense. As a result, your mind becomes purified and you get the most out of life. You may not be very wealthy, very powerful and famous, but you will enjoy life in the true sense because your mind will be peaceful and balanced. And whatever material possession or position you may have in life, you will get the most out of it.

As a result, you will understand the inherent limitation of this life. You will know this life, however glorious and fascinating it may be, cannot satisfy man's inner longing for complete freedom from all bondage and suffering, man's inner longing for immortality. You must understand that this is the relative order where opposites coexist—life and death, growth and decay, smile and tears, hope and fear, knowledge and ignorance. Here there is no hope of joy and unmixed blessing. This world is constituted of dualities; it cannot be made perfect. But it can be used as an instrument, as a means to perfection: "Know the truth and the truth shall make you free", said Jesus Christ. This is one of the truths, that the world consists of dualities. Beyond this is the absolute—there is perfection and that perfection is God. God is man's highest ideal of perfection. There is no immortality anywhere else but in God. There is no perfection anywhere else but in God. There is no real freedom anywhere else but in God. There is no absolute goodness anywhere else but in God. A person called Jesus Christ, "Good Master." Jesus answered, "Why do you call me good? God alone is good." A great truth in the absolute sense.

In this world there is only relative good. From one standpoint you will consider something good, but from another standpoint you may consider it bad. From one standpoint kindness is good, but kindness cannot exist unless

HOW TO PURIFY THE MIND

there is concomitant evil somewhere. Justice cannot exist unless there is wrongdoing somewhere. The human mind cannot be satisfied with this kind of ideal. If you follow moral principles as values in themselves, you eventually come to realize that you are seeking something beyond the dualities. What is that? It is the search for the eternal, the search for God.

Religion is the only pursuit that is specially concerned with the eternal. It holds the promise to you of eternal life, or absolute peace and blessedness. This worldly life does not hold out to you a promise even of the fulfilment of your legitimate desires and hopes. Yet still you hanker after perfection in this world. When you become disillusioned with the nature of the world, then you will seek God. Everything in this life—your wealth, your virtue, your pleasure, intellectual or aesthetic—can serve as instrumental to the attainment of the highest, but none of these can be an end in itself.

When you are disillusioned you accept this life as a means, as preparatory to the attainment of the highest. You cannot be indifferent to this life or ignore it. All this while you thought you would eventually find complete self-fulfilment in this life; now you come to realize that everything in this life has instrumental value only, that God is the one absolute, ultimate value. You change your position and find that you are developing an awareness of God, and that this universe is not the whole of reality. You become aware of the presence of God, and you understand that He is the sole master of the world, and of your ego, and then you surrender to Him. You dedicate everything to Him. From disillusionment you come to dispassion. The moment you consider this world as the means to the highest end, you are more or less detached. But this does not mean indifference. You hold to this world as a means and the attainment of the goal depends on the proper use of the means. You use this life for the best purpose, the attainment of the highest : God.

Through the practice of virtue we have come to the first landmark, which is purification of the mind. The second landmark is disillusionment with the world. Then you reach the third landmark, which is living with dispassion in this world. You dedicate yourself to God and live in this world as a custodian, as a caretaker. That is the only position you hold in this life. You do your duties, taking care of everything you should. As a result, the mind is more and more

HOW TO PURIFY THE MIND 41

purified. This is the practice of karma yoga. You work with dispassion, doing duties with dispassion, looking upon this life as a means to the attainment of the transcendental reality.

Gradually, your mind is purified and you develop a natural longing for God realization. But, so far, you have exercised your power of calculation. You think, yes, I understand the drawbacks of this life, but your heart must join with the intellect. If you continue your spiritual practice, then your heart will join with the intellect, and you develop a longing for God realization. It is not just through calculation or argumentation that you understand this truth, now you have a genuine longing for it. With this longing comes an inwardness of the mind. You understand that God is the innermost reality, the very essence of the universe.

Everything transitory contains the absolute. Nothing can be annihilated, not a single grain of dust or a single grain of sand can be annihilated. This absolute, the Supreme Being, dwells within each and every individual as the central principle of consciousness. That you really are! This idea develops within. You become fully aware of the existence of God, and you know that God is not far away, that He dwells within as the innermost Self; that divine essence is within you. You understand that the supreme value is not outside, but inside. You develop an inwardness of mind. The outward tendency, constantly seeking self-fulfilment in the sense objects, is counteracted by the inward tendency. You think of reality as the underlying being holding the universe.

With inwardness of the mind, work is no longer compulsory for you; that is, work is not necessary for your inner development anymore. If you give up external duties—of course, your situation in life must permit it—and apply yourself only to spiritual disciplines, it is not wrong. If you have many obligations, that is a different situation. Sri Ramakrishna used to give an illustration: If you have a wound, a scab is formed as the wound heals. If you take off the scab by force, it delays the healing of the wound, but when the wound heals from within, the scab drops off. Similarly, all the duties with which you are preoccupied, these duties so binding, are not binding anymore. You develop real devotion, longing for God, and at this stage you can take to more spiritual pursuits. Free from the obligation to society to a great extent, you can carry on mental, physical, and verbal worship as much as possible. Gradually, the *samskaras*, the

HOW TO PURIFY THE MIND 43

impressions of wrong deeds, will be eliminated to a great extent, and then devotion will grow. When true devotion grows in the mind, the mind becomes absorbed in God. Only then does meditation become effective.

According to many religions of the world, one practice is very effective: the repetition of the name of God. This is a kind of universal practice, and you can practise it wherever you go. This practice is common among Christians, Buddhists, Mohammedans, and Hindus. Here you are dealing with the subtler impurities of the mind. When Jesus Christ said, "Blessed are the pure in heart, for they shall see God," he meant complete purification of the mind. Not only gross impurities must be removed from the mind, but the subtlest impurities must also be removed from the mind—then one can see God.

One very effective way of removing these subtle impurities is the repetition of God's name. Sri Krishna gives an illustration: Suppose a lump of gold is brought to you. If there is dust on it, you remove it by wiping. If there is some stain, you remove it by washing. But if there are impurities within this alloy, you cannot extract them so easily. You have to put it in fire, then the impurities are smelted out and completely separated from the gold, because the impurities are not inherent in the gold. In a similar manner, impurities are drawn out of the mind from the subconscious level, and the process for this smelting of the mind comes through the repetition of the sacred word or name.

I recall one experience I had when I met a Mohammedan teacher. He was living on a houseboat on the river. We heard a Mohammedan saint had come. We didn't have any prejudice against any saint, because all the saints belong to God, so we went to see him one evening. One of his followers asked the saint a question. Even when he was talking with us he was counting the rosary, so one of us asked him the question: "Why do you count the rosary?" He said: "For cleansing different things there are different materials and processes. If you want to cleanse the floor you adopt one method. If you want to clean the walls, the woodwork or the windows, you adopt other methods. For cleansing the mind, also, I have found some process. I have a sacred formula and I repeat this—that is the soap I am constantly applying. It is the best soap I have found for cleansing the mind."

Hindus, Buddhists, Sufis, and many Christians also emphasize this process. Just as there are different ailments in this life, there are different medicines and remedies for each kind of ailment. For the ailment of impurities in the mind, the repetition of the sacred name or formula has been found to be the best remedy. So a person must continue the process. When his mind is further purified and natural devotion, deep devotion, grows within the heart, then he can practise meditation on God successfully. The mind becomes completely absorbed, so much so that the mind becomes suffused with the light of the Divinity, and perception of God comes.

Our progress in life from whatever level, up to the highest attainment of God, depends on the purification of the mind. There are various methods of purification according to our stage in life and our situation. According to our capacities, we can adopt these methods and ultimately purify the mind to such an extent that we can be perfect as the Father in Heaven is perfect. ❑

3. THE MIND AND THE SOUL

The physical body, the mind, and the soul, are three distinct factors of the human personality. They are vitally connected and appear to be one single entity, but, truly speaking, they are distinguishable and can even be separated.

According to many psychologists and philosophers, the physical body is all-in-all. They do not acknowledge the existence of mind or the soul as separate entities, believing that consciousness is just a function of the brain. Many used to think that just as the liver secretes bile, so the brain secretes thoughts. According to the behaviourists, thinking is silent talk. Even Professor James thought that our emotions are only the results of physical activity. For instance, all of a sudden you see a tiger in the way, and you take to your heels. Fear supposedly results from this movement of the body. These psychologists and philosophers believe that what we call

THE MIND AND THE SOUL

thought, emotion, imagination, and memory are simply derived from physical and chemical responses in the body.

If we analyse the facts of life, we have to recognize the existence of mind as a distinct principle from the physical body. According to Vedanta, mind is *antahkarana*, the internal instrument. We have five external instruments of perception: eyes, ears, nose, the organ of touch, the organ of taste. Similarly, we have the internal instrument for internal perception. For instance, happiness, fear, hope, pride, hatred—all these are events. You perceive these internal events by an inner instrument called the mind. If we do not acknowledge the inner perception as the criterion of reality, we cannot establish such events as happiness, hope, fear, pride, as realities. Just as an external object, a chair for example, is a reality, similarly, your happiness, your hope, your fear, your pride, are also realities.

You cannot demonstrate your love simply by its physical expression. Love is different from its physical expression, just as happiness is different from its physical expression. You may welcome a friend to your home, but you may not be happy to see him, yet you can receive him with a smile and sweet words. These are the physical expressions of happiness, although you are not happy. Inner happiness is something different from the outer expression. Similarly, you may not love a person, still, you can embrace him, speak sweet words, give him a nice present. So, we find what we call love is something different from the physical expression. Unless we recognize the inner perception, we cannot recognize love as a fact of life. But love is a fact of life, so inner perception is also a fact, and the instrument of inner perception is mind.

We see things with the external instruments, yet they alone are not adequate for perception. The mind is necessary, not only for internal perception, but for external perception also. For instance, you are looking at a person, seeing him and hearing his words. But, if your mind is elsewhere, though your ears are not plugged with cotton, you will not hear his words. The words will enter the ears, strike the tympanum, but there will be no reaction from within. Your eyes may receive the impression of the person—the brain is connected to the optic nerve and the eardrums—still, there may not be a response. There is no dissociation physically speaking, yet there is something lacking because of which you cannot hear or see the person even

THE MIND AND THE SOUL

though your ears and your eyes are open. What is that lack? It is something that can be distinguished from this physical system. It is the mind. But with that mind you can watch the reaction you have within to the other person's ideas, and decide whether you approve of them or not. Externally, you see the person, and internally, you watch the reactions to that person within yourself. That by which you watch the reactions, that is the mind.

The mind has other functions also. When we see a thing, it is registered somewhere in this system, and we judge it. We do not simply receive perceptions, we evaluate things intellectually, morally, aesthetically. The eyes receive an impression of a person, and, at the same time, you judge that person. He may be physically a very handsome person, still, you may not value him very highly. Intellectually, he may be short of the standard, fall short morally also. This evaluation is not done by the eyes. You hear music, and you judge by a different measure. There is much more in the physical system than that which the eyes and ears register. You have an instrument for judging things physically, intellectually, morally, aesthetically. That instrument is the mind, which is distinct from the physical system.

There is another reason why we think mind is not identical with the physical body. You can very closely distinguish between mental and physical pain. You know, when there is heartache within you, whether it is within the physical or psychical heart. If there are problems within you, such as frustration or rebellion, you don't go to a medical doctor, you go to a psychiatrist. How do you make such a clear-cut distinction between physical and psychical pain? It would not be possible if the mind was an aspect of the physical system. By speaking just a few short words in your ear, I can give you a tremendous mental shock without hurting your body in the least. How is this possible? These facts point to the truth that the mind is not identical with the physical body. We have also seen persons who are physically very sound, yet, they are idiots. Probably, no doctor could find anything wrong, even in the structure of their brain, yet they are imbeciles. Apparently, there is a distinct principle such as the mind which is different from the physical body.

The mind has different functions such as cognition, emotion, and volition. Of these functions, cognition is the primary or basic function. The system of Vedanta has particularly analysed

THE MIND AND THE SOUL

the function of cognition, and finds this cognition is a fourfold process. In the beginning you have indeterminate knowledge of a thing that presents itself to your vision. Then comes another function which calls forth memory. For instance, a thing like a chair appears to you. You call forth the impression stored within you. You say: "Yes, it is similar to that impression from long ago which I called a chair. So this is a chair." So you have gone through the third stage of determination, or decision. Then you relate the mental picture you have within to some particular existing mental impression and you say, "I know it is a chair." So these are the four functions of the mind in determining an object. First of all, there was an indeterminate state called *manas*, then the memory state called *chitta*, followed by the determinative state called *buddhi*, and finally came the stage of egoism called *ahamkara* "I know."

The mind is not actually the very centre of the human personality. There is another factor, which is called *soul*, *Atman*, or *Self*. Many philosophers and psychologists do not distinguish between mind and soul. Truly speaking, in Western thought, soul has not been very much differentiated from the mind. In Hindu psychology the Self is always differentiated from the mind, because the mind is not the real experiencer or perceiver of mental phenomenon. Because the functions of the mind are also observed, the mind falls into the category of the object. Therefore, it is something different from the subject, the knower, the perceiver. You can watch your mental movements, but you are someone different from the happenings in the mind. The argument is sometimes made that the mind can be the subject as well as the object. Why is another entity acknowledged as the observer of the mind? The answer is that the subject and object are contrary. The object is something that does not have consciousness as its very essence. The subject is that which knows, perceives, and has consciousness as its very essence. This is the essential difference between the subject and the object, the knower and the known. Anything that falls into the category of the known does not have consciousness as its very essence, while the subject does. Now if mind is essentially material, insentient, it cannot be the subject; these two are contrary and cannot form one entity. They cannot be joined together. Matter and spirit can be vitally associated, but cannot form one entity, a single principle. There-

THE MIND AND THE SOUL

fore, the knower, the experiencer, must be distinct from the mind.

Patanjali says that mind is not the Self because mind is the observed; the Self is the observer. Some philosophers argue: "All right, let there be the observer called Self, ego, but what guarantee is there that this ego-self is an unchanging principle? There may be a fluctuating ego. I see, I hear, I stand, I speak, I eat, I sleep, I dream; there may be a continual flow of ego-selves. There is no necessity of acknowledging a permanent Self abiding through all these experiences." Even William James did not harbour the idea of the permanent abiding Self.

A Buddhist teacher, Nagasena, who lived in the third century A.D. did not acknowledge the existence of the permanent ego. He said that this whole physical system is a continuous stream of physical and psychical elements. There is no integrating principle, permanent, abiding, that integrates all the psychical and physical elements into a coherent whole. Even up to the modern day, some modern philosophers and psychologists do not acknowledge any Self at all. And those that do acknowledge something as the ego-self do not acknowledge it to be something abiding. We find that Hume had the same idea.

He said, "I do not see any one permanent thing. It is a constantly changing string of egos." Professor Stout, the founder of some essential points of knowledge, also held the same idea. Russell also does not acknowledge any Self because it is not observable. We observe only fluctuating egos, the eating I, the feeling I, the thinking I, the knowing I, the seeing I, but no permanent, unchanging "I" do we perceive. It cannot be perceived, it cannot be observed, because it is the observer of all that is observed. The answer was given by the Upanishadic saints centuries ago: "That which is the ultimate knower, That which is behind all these fluctuating sense objects, by what can you know That, see That?" That cannot be objectified because it is the ultimate seer: there is nothing behind That.

Observation implies an observer. Experience implies an experiencer. That which is the ultimate experiencer, through which everything is seen and observed, cannot be observed by anything else. If it could be observed, it would fall into the category of the observed, and one would need another observer to establish it as a fact. There is one ultimate observer of all observation and experience. That is the Self. Consciousness is the very basis of thought. It cannot

THE MIND AND THE SOUL

be an object of thought or cognition. Consciousness, Self, is the very basis of cognition. It cannot be objectified.

If you do not acknowledge the permanent Self, you cannot establish the existence of memory. Knowledge is the relation of the present experiences with the past experiences. For example, you see a person. You know at once that this is the same person you saw yesterday. That is, you link your present experience with the experience you had yesterday. But if the Self that saw the person yesterday had already gone and, another Self has come today, then how could you relate the two experiences? William James gives an answer: all of these egos are like beads, strung on a string one after another continually. When one ego passes, then that ego imparts to its successor what it had. Now the question is, if everything is momentary, then how can the past ego pass anything to the succeeding ego? Unless that exists at the same time, the predecessor cannot pass anything to the succeeding ego. They must coexist at least two moments. Then James's idea fails. He contends that when the ego of this moment dies, the ego of the second moment comes. If this be your contention, then the theory that the predecessor passes something to the successor cannot hold good. This is the argument Shankara gave against the Buddhist theory of momentariness. The Buddhists used to say that if you take a ball of fire and swing it around, you will see a wheel of fire. They held the same idea about memory: one passes something to a successor. How can you do this unless the predecessor and the successor exist at the same time? You say one dies and another comes. It is a continuous flow. Continuity implies something underlying, otherwise continuity does not mean anything; it is all disconnected egos. If one is composed of all disconnected egos there cannot be memory or knowledge in the true sense. If you say that there is continuity, there must be something permanent, abiding, unchanging—the Self. Vedanta states that when you say, "I think, I feel, I imagine," it does not mean that separate "I"s think, feel, and imagine. There are not many "I"s, only one. The same "I" that thinks also feels or imagines. There is one "I" that, when connected with the particular function, sees, feels, and so on.

Suppose you tell me something about a house. Then I go and see the house. At once, I recognize, yes, this is the house I was told about. If the "I" that heard about the house yesterday is

THE MIND AND THE SOUL

different from the "I" that sees the house today, you could not say that you heard about the house yesterday. That means that the same "I" that heard through the ears, is the same "I" that is seeing the house through the eyes. It is not two different "I"s. The same entity functions through the ears and the eyes. The eyes do not see, the ears do not hear. Something beyond the eyes, beyond the ears, exists yesterday and today. That something heard through the ears yesterday, and today it sees through the eyes and recognizes the house.

Patanjali says that had this Self been changing, changes could not be registered. The very fact of change presupposes a permanent experiencer. We experience changes continually. If the perceiver of changes itself changed, then it could not experience changes. For instance, here is an arrangement of food. Now you see it and then you leave the room. When you come back, if there has been any change in the arrangement, you cannot know it if you are not the same person. How can you know it? If the experiencer changes, then he cannot know what change there has been. If you are the same person, then you will recognize there has been a change in the arrangement. If the experiencer changes continually with the changes in the external world, he cannot know the external world. The fact that we know changes inside and outside shows that the experiencer can relate the previous conditions to the succeeding condition and, by comparing, the individual knows change. The very fact that there is change in the world and change in the mind within shows that the experiencer is unchanging.

There is one unchanging, abiding Self, and that Self, being essentially the knower, the experiencer, is of the nature of Pure Consciousness: self-shining, self-luminous, the Light of all lights. There is a light that is beyond all physical lights, beyond the light of the senses, beyond the light of the mind. That is the Light of the Self, unchanging, which is distinct from this ego. Even when the ego subsides, that Light remains as a passive witness. There is one Self that is beyond all changing conditions, external and internal. Somehow or other, that Self has been associated with the psychophysical system, which is so mixed up that it doesn't realize the Self as it really is. When you realize the Self you know you are absolutely free, pure, immortal.

You must recognize you are the very ruler of the psychophysical system. You became a

THE MIND AND THE SOUL

slave of this because you became identified with it. You cannot control the body and the mind simply because you do not know how to assert yourself as the master of the psychophysical system. The moment you know you are only the dweller in this psychophysical system, you become master of your senses. The moment you know you are distinct from the body and the mind, you are self-luminous, eternal, undecaying, unchanging Principle, divine in nature, ever associated with the Divine Being. At once purity will come to you, strength will come to you, hope will come to you, joy will come to you. This is the whole secret of true development.

Vedanta says again and again, know this Self and let all vanity go away. Know the Self. Realize the Self. When you know your Self, you at once realize your essential unity with the Divine Being, because you find the Self that is luminous, self-existent, pure, free, painless, deathless, free from decay, the Self that is not confined within this psychophysical system. That Self is actually united with the Supreme Self that pervades the whole universe.

At present you die and are reborn simply because you think of yourself as the physical body. You think you are sick because you identify yourself with the physical body. You simply delude yourself with the idea, I am dark or fair, young or old, unhappy or happy. All that is delusion. The Self is ever pure, free, immortal. The moment you realize this, you are free, absolutely free. You are transported to the realm of the Supreme Spirit that pervades the whole universe. We live in Him, we move in Him, we have our whole being in Him. But just as blind people, living and moving in the full blaze of the noonday sun, do not know the splendour of the midday sun, we do not know it. We exist because of that Supreme Reality, self-shining. We do not know Him simply because of blindness. This has to be overcome by recognition of the Self as it is. Day and night remember that you are related to the Supreme Being. Assert yourself as you are and everything will be right. When the president comes to the assembly, at once it comes to order. When the Divine Being asserts itself in this psychophysical system, the whole system will be in order. Gradually, darkness will leave you, and you will realize your unity with the Divine Being. ❑

4. THE MIND AND ITS WAYS

The importance of the human mind cannot be overestimated. Mind is the cause of bondage and also the cause of freedom. If the mind is well cared for, trained and developed, then it becomes the way to complete freedom. But if the mind is uncared for, untrained and undeveloped, then one remains in bondage. Our happiness and unhappiness, knowledge and ignorance, success and failure, strength and weakness depend on the nature of the mind. Our outer achievements are but a manifestation of our inner attainments. It is because of the superiority of the mind that humanity is superior to all other living creatures. So the question arises—what is the nature of this mind? How can we manipulate it?

There are differences of opinion among philosophers of the East and West as to the true nature of the mind. According to Vedanta, the mind occupies an intermediate position between the knowing Self and the body. This physical body is not the whole of human personality. Within this physical body dwells the Self, and that Self is the centre of human personality. That central principle in human personality coordinates all the functions of the organs and integrates all the physical and mental factors into a coherent whole.

We cannot say the eyes see, ears hear, the hands work, the mouth tastes, the nose smells, because there are not that many rulers in the psychophysical system. There is one central Self, the knower within, that sees through the eyes, that hears through the ears, that works with the hands, that tastes through the mouth, that smells through the nose. Thus a person says, I see, I hear, I work, I taste, I smell—one central factor. Despite the changing functions, this remains constant. This knowing Self dwelling within the body is the seer, and it is the hearer, it smells, it tastes, it thinks, it determines, it is the doer and it is the knowing Self, the knower within. This knower within knows the external objects, this knower within also knows the physical conditions—whether you are dark or fair, whether you are young or old, you know because you are distinct from the objects known. The knower is

THE MIND AND ITS WAYS 63

always distinct from what is known. They are of contrary nature. Consciousness as its essence belongs to the knower, never to the known. Like light and darkness, they are of contrary nature, so one cannot be identified with the other. Knower is knower, the known is known.

Besides these functions of seeing, hearing, feeling, tasting or smelling, man has other functions. He can think, feel, will, imagine, remember, and so forth. What do these functions belong to? Each of the organs is capable of a particular function. You walk with the legs and not with the hands, you see through the eyes and not through the ears, you hear through the ears and not through the eyes. Each of these organs has its respective function.

You think, feel, will, imagine, remember, yet none of the external organs is responsible for these functions. Your organs may be still, your body may be quiet, yet you think, feel, imagine, remember. You cannot attribute these functions to any of the external organs—organs of perception, organs of action—none of the ten organs can be responsible for these functions. These functions cannot be explained as physical processes. These functions have consciousness implicit in them. Do you think a chair can think or feel or imagine? We can move it from one place to another, it may break, disintegrate, but it cannot think, feel or imagine because it is a material substance. Thinking, feeling, imagining, remembering requires consciousness, sentience. The functions associated with or having consciousness inherent in them cannot be explained as physical processes. These functions, being charged with consciousness, cannot be explained simply as functions of the physical organs, or the body, or the brain, which is part of the physical body.

In Western philosophy mind is either identified with the subject, or is associated with the physical body. Many philosophers and psychologists have explained mental functions as physical processes. According to some, mind is a series of conscious functions derived from physical processes. There have been philosophers, even a great philosopher like Leibnitz, who say that the mind is the subject; it thinks, feels, and imagines. But no, the mind is not the subject. The subject is distinct; the knower is distinct from the mind. The mind occupies an intermediate position between the real knower and the body.

Broadly speaking, there are three principal factors of human being: the real knower, the mind, and the body. The mind is associated with the functions of the organs. But the knower and the organs are not totally responsible for perception. You are looking at a person, you are hearing his words, yet suddenly you fail to hear him—or even see him. He asks you what happened and you tell him you were inattentive, you were absent-minded. This shows that you, the knower, and your organs, such as the eyes, the ears, are not solely responsible for perception. If these eyes and the knower within are adequate for perception there would have always been perception. But there is a third factor which receives and that is the mind.

The mind is responsible for action also. If you are distracted and your mind is agitated or bewildered, can you do anything? Can you cook a dinner when your mind is bewildered? You cannot do anything. You may not be able even to stand. Then, behind the organs of perception, behind the organs of action, there is another factor of the mind: the power of introspection.

Mind is responsible for external functions, and it is also responsible for inner perception. A person's joy and sorrow, hope and fear, love and hate, are directly known to that person alone. We cannot study them directly through that person's external behaviour. Yet through a person's external behaviour you can judge the internal feelings. This, however, is the indirect way of knowing. Each person can know directly whether he or she is happy or not, whether she has love or hatred towards anybody. But you cannot know through outer behaviour only. If you ask a woman: "Do you love your husband?" She may answer: "Yes, I love him. I speak sweetly to him. I hug him and kiss him." But these actions do not guarantee that she loves him. She may or may not love him. She knows that she loves him not through her external behaviour, but through her inner feeling, her inner perception. Just as external perception is the criterion of reality, similarly inner perception is the criterion of reality. For this inner perception, mind is the instrument. We cannot deny this. If we deny this, we cannot establish the reality of love and hate, joy and sorrow. We cannot establish the reality of hope and fear. These are real because you directly perceive them. Each person knows these things directly. The mind is responsible for this. But consciousness is not intrinsic to the mind.

Consciousness belongs to the knower behind all perception. This mind, its functions and

THE MIND AND ITS WAYS

its states, do not belong to the physical body, they belong to something else. Your mental distress and physical distress are not identical. The mind is distinguished from the knower, and because mind falls into the category of the known, mind cannot have consciousness inherent in it. Anything that has no consciousness intrinsic to it is material, according to Vedanta.

What is self-luminous, has consciousness intrinsic to it, is pure spirit. Anything else is material. But though mind is material in the sense that it has no consciousness as its essence, it does have the power to transmit consciousness. Just as glass can transmit light, or a glass ball can be transparent through light, or just as an iron ball can be aglow with fire and can keep light and heat, similarly, the mind has the capacity to transmit consciousness, which belongs as its essence to the real Self. Mind has that capacity, and, because of that, mind is the chief instrument of cognition. Anything you know, you know through the mind.

The sense organs alone are not responsible for perception. The mind must be associated with each sense organ in order to make it capable of perception. Even actions are not possible unless the mind is associated with them, because it is consciousness that is really responsible for all our actions and all our thoughts. The human body is characteristically inert, just as anything that is material is characteristically inert, devoid of all action. Whatever action is possible in living creatures is due to consciousness imparted to the physical system through the mind. The mind is the chief instrument of knowledge. Anything we know, we know through the mind, from the grossest to the subtlest, from the lowest to the highest.

Mind has many different functions, the principal of which are cognition, volition, and emotion. According to Vedanta, cognition is basic: it underlies volition and emotion. One cannot feel or will without cognition. Unless you know the object that you desire to have, you cannot be attached to it; you cannot have love or hatred with regard to it.

Cognition, according to Vedanta, has four main functions: deliberation, determination, memory, and egoism. The two main functions are determination and deliberation. Before you determine something and come to a particular decision, you go through a stage of deliberation. But determination, reaching a conclusion or decision, is very important because it requires rea-

THE MIND AND ITS WAYS

soning and understanding. Unless you have the power to discriminate between right and wrong, apparent and real, you cannot come to a decision.

The mind is associated with each perception, whether auditory, or any other perception, but the mind's function does not end at that point. There is another reason why Vedanta acknowledges the existence of mind as a distinct principle: mind cannot be explained away just as a process, or a state, or an attribute. It is a substance to which these processes and attributes belong. The organs are responsible more or less for the presentation of the thing, but mind, apart from being responsible for presentation is also responsible for judgment of things. You taste some food and your organ of taste says, "Oh, it is so delicious." Then you stop eating even though you know it to be delicious. It is delicious, but it is not wholesome. You may see a person, he may appear very attractive to the eye, but still the mind decides, "No, he is not a desirable companion." The organs are responsible for the manifestation of the objects, but the mind is responsible for judging the object. It is mind and mind alone that can differentiate between good and pleasant.

A child will say that anything pleasant is good. This is the conclusion of immature minds. It is a great tragedy of life that what is attractive and what is pleasant is not necessarily good. This tragedy becomes more manifest as a person grows in years. It is the *buddhi*, the determinative function of the mind, that has the capacity to judge pros and cons of things and find that which is most desirable. It can contemplate the possible courses in a certain situation and determine the one that is to be followed. The role of the will is to accomplish the purpose of buddhi. Buddhi, the determining faculty, will tell you, "Yes, this is the right thing and that is the wrong thing," and it will stop there. Then you will say, "Yes, this is the right course to follow," and volition will come.

In most individuals there is a cleavage between their rational and emotional natures. Truly speaking, moral life depends on bridging the gap between rationality and the emotions. Reason says something is the wrong thing, yet our emotions will not listen to the warning of reason. With effort, will-power, we pull back our emotions and align them with reason. This is the struggle that is involved in rational life. By repeated effort—there is no other way—and with

THE MIND AND ITS WAYS

firm will, we can align the emotional nature with the rational nature and bridge the gap.

Vedanta maintains a priority of reason: without right decision there cannot be right action. Will must be guided by reason. But there is a difficulty in that. Reason will not develop unless the mind is purified to a certain extent. When reason is developed, reason can say, "Yes, that is right" or, "No, that is wrong." However, in most human beings reason is not well developed, while the emotions are already developed. Emotions pull you here and there, what can we do? In the beginning, the only course is to depend on authority. Persons with superior reasoning power will have to make the decisions. Before a child develops reasoning power, his emotions, which are already developed, will tear him apart if he is left to his own devices. If, in the name of "self-expression", a child is permitted to follow his or her own way, they will end up under the control of government laws, or the police force, or the military force. They will, in their immaturity, try to escape authority in the name of self expression, and will end up controlled by social laws. Until human beings find some scope for the development of reason, you cannot leave them to their own judgment.

There are factors in man's psychophysical constitution, such as bad habits, wrong tendencies, sense desires, passions, and prejudices that often can vitiate his judgment, and retard his power of action. Undesirable emotions prevail against the remonstrance of reason and the resistance of will. This is why it is necessary to develop both reason and will by all possible measures. There should not be licentiousness in the name of liberty. By the exercise of his reason and will in every situation, as far as possible, a person can get rid of his weaknesses. There are positive courses by which one can cultivate the powers of reason and will. Persistent effort in the right direction despite repeated failures is the secret of every great achievement. There is nothing man cannot accomplish by his indomitable will, joined with clear and keen understanding. If a person succeeds in developing reason then his emotional nature naturally comes under control, as does his moral nature. In this case moral behaviour is an expression of inner nature, or inner consciousness. Such a person need not be controlled; such a person can have freedom of action and need not be under authority. The law may or may not exist for them, for the law is not for the virtuous but for the wicked.

THE MIND AND ITS WAYS

Virtuous people do not need any law or regulation.

Subduing the senses does not mean the suppression of sense desires, but the overcoming and outgrowing of them by limiting experiences and by giving the mind a higher direction. It is freedom of will that demarcates the human from the subhuman. In the subhuman level instinct prevails. On the human level, reason prevails, and the volition associated with reason is the determining factor on the human level. So this work with volition, guided by reason, is called *karma*.

Volitional action is a special privilege of human life. Man has the capacity to judge rightly or wrongly, and he has the capacity to follow his judgment, rightly or wrongly. This power is called *karma*. This is why human life is called the *karma-bhumi*, the level of volitional action, generally speaking. Whatever a person does with any of the organs or with the body or with the mind, leaves an impression on the mind. These impressions do not always dwell on the surface of the mind; they may go to a lower level of the mind. We can see very little of our mind. All of our thoughts, ideas, feelings, and memories are not always manifest on the surface of the mind.

Some emotion, thought, idea, or vision may prevail within you now, but in a few minutes you may lose it. Where did it go? There is another level of the mind where these things go. You distinguish these two levels in this way: whatever is manifest to your waking ego is the conscious level. Its range is very limited. What is below this range of ego-consciousness is the subconscious level. We get impressions through all of our volitional actions and these impressions gravitate to the lower level and rest there.

These impressions, according to the sage Patanjali, live in different ways. Everything that you know is not manifest within you at once. Our emotions, thoughts, feelings, ideas, are sometimes manifest and sometimes unmanifest, these that are unmanifest dwell in the subconscious level. There are many that are dormant; many powers or talents may be dormant in the child, and develop as the child grows. The impressions that are dormant within us do not influence the conscious mind. But there are others that may become overpowered, for instance, when there is a calamity. Some wrong desires and passions may be overpowered under stressful circumstances or feelings. They, more or less, influence the conscious level.

THE MIND AND ITS WAYS

If you have some wrong tendencies and yet you associate with good people, if you do not believe in God and still you associate with believers of God, gradually your disbelief in God becomes attenuated. If you have an antipathy toward religion, that antipathy can also be gradually eliminated. Many wrong tendencies can be eliminated through culture and education. Our wrong tendencies gradually become eliminated by contrary efforts. One of the ways of overcoming wrong tendencies is to try to cultivate positive tendencies in the conscious state. Vedanta always stresses the conscious level of the mind because it is on the conscious level that volition and will function. Whatever you gain, you gain through the right exercise of will. Man's development in any level of life—intellectual, aesthetic, moral, or spiritual—depends on culture. There is no intellectual or aesthetic level in the lower creatures, but man lives on different levels. Man's progress in life on the different levels depends on culture. Culture in this sense means systematic effort with volition guided by reason. A person has to develop through the exercise of will, guided by reason.

If a person has a strong tendency to oppress others, he can work to overcome it by trying to help others as much as possible. You have to have a little recognition of your weakness, then association with the right types of persons and constant effort in the other direction will cure it. As Patanjali says, "If you want to overcome the wrong tendencies, your subconscious level cannot take care of you. This is accomplished on the conscious level where reasoning and volition function." You determine what is contrary to the problem and move in that direction. Vedanta always stresses the importance of the conscious level. While it is true that the subconscious urges can be very strong, the fight against those urges must be fought on the conscious level.

Every person is born with a particular psychophysical constitution that one brings from one's previous incarnation. The impressions dwell at the subconscious level; and when a person dies he simply drops the physical body, and carries along the mind with all its traits. In course of time these traits develop with the emotional nature developing first, even before reason grows. That is why children and young people should be under the authority of superior judgment. All these three—reason, volition, and emotion—are essential to human life, but both volition and emotion should be guided by rea-

THE MIND AND ITS WAYS

son. In the early years, reason will not develop because the mind has to be purified to a certain extent by the observance of moral principles. Emotions are not wrong in themselves, but they need the guidance of reason. They are right or wrong according to the direction in which they move. That very desire for sense objects that causes delusion, bondage, and suffering, when turned Godward changes into divine love and leads to liberation, peace, and blessedness perpetual.

A devotee steeped in Hindu tradition will pray to the Lord: "That undying love which the unwise have for the objects of the senses, may that love never leave my heart as I meditate on Thee." That same love, that greed, that which you may call passion, can be turned into devotion to God just by changing the direction of the mind. The same water has different characteristics when it flows through different channels. Water can kill, yet the same water can save a person's life, not because there is a difference in the essential nature of the water, but because of the extraneous matter that gets mixed with the water. Mind, according to Vedanta, is made of pure substance. We may despair of controlling the mind because of its restlessness. We may think that the mind can never be made quiet, but it is not so. Mind has restlessness because of the impressions that have gathered within us. These impressions, particularly those of an emotional nature, are of the nature of attachment and aversion, and they cause restlessness. Actually, the mind has a natural tendency to be calm, but these adverse forces within us make the mind move, oscillate, and waver. The more the mind is purified, the more the mind becomes calm, and in the calm mind there is knowledge. The calm mind is capable of being concentrated, and knowledge grows through concentration of the mind.

Reason has vision but cannot act; emotion can act but has no vision. If reason rides on the shoulders of emotion, they can get along very well. Even wrong emotions have not to be crushed; they can be transformed or sublimated. As pointed out by Sri Ramakrishna, they can be turned into good account by changing their course. Instead of hating others, one should hate one's own weaknesses. Instead of being angry with another's failures, one should be angry with one's own failures. Instead of being proud of transitory possessions, one should be proud of one's divine heritage and refrain from doing anything unbecoming. Instead of being jealous of the worldly-minded, one should be jealous of the devotees of God and make a sincere effort to emulate them.

Emotions make life zestful. Devoid of love or fellow-feeling or regard, great achievements through reason and volition alone are but mechanical performances. Intellect can enlighten the way but cannot give inspiration, which comes from the heart. What man needs is the combination of head and heart. Swami Vivekananda says:

> What we really want is head and heart combined. The heart is great indeed; it is through the heart that come the great inspirations of life. I would a hundred times rather have a little heart and no brain, than be all brains and no heart. Life is possible, progress is possible for him who has heart, but he who has no heart and only brains dies of dryness.
>
> At the same time we know that he who is carried along by his heart alone has to undergo many ills, for now and then he is liable to tumble into pitfalls. The combination of heart and head is what we want. I do not mean that a man should compromise his heart for his brain or vice versa, but let everyone have

an infinite amount of heart and feeling, and at the same time an infinite amount of reason. Is there any limit to what we want in this world? Is not the world infinite? There is room for an infinite amount of feeling, and so also for an infinite amount of culture and reason. Let them come together without limit, let them be running together, as it were, in parallel lines each with the other.*

When the mind becomes pure and the emotions are controlled, the volition is guided and reason develops. When ethical conduct becomes natural, then the mind remains calm under varying conditions of life, and a person can really get the power of concentration. He can then meditate on anything he wants. This meditation or concentration is the secret of knowledge, secular and spiritual.

In the interest of both secular and spiritual pursuits it is necessary that the mind should be calm; but the mind will never be calm unless it is purified to a certain extent. The practice of virtue is essential for secular development as well as for spiritual development. If man wants the

The Complete Works of Swami Vivekananda, Vol.II Mayavati Memorial Edition (10th Edition), 1963, Advaita Ashrama, Calcutta, India, p.145.

THE MIND AND ITS WAYS

highest, it is through concentration of the mind that he has to attain the highest. Devotion to God grows in a purified mind, and when there is devotion in the mind, the mind becomes settled on God, and then regulation comes.

This is how the mind functions. Through purifying the mind the different activities of the mind are harmonized. Through purification of the mind, reason and volition are developed, and control over the emotions is attained. Whether you want physical, intellectual, aesthetic or spiritual development, purification of the mind is an essential condition. Through purification of the mind, you can achieve what you want.

Any kind of greatness requires right understanding, the exercise of volition, and the control of the emotions through right understanding. Through these one attains the purification of the mind, and through the purification of the mind, he attains the highest goal of life. ❑

5. THE MIND AND THE SENSES

The mind and the senses are very important factors of the human personality, because all our knowledge depends on them. We have one mind and five senses. The senses are the faculties of the five bodily organs. We have the faculty of seeing because of the organ of vision that we call the eyes. We have the faculty of hearing because of the organ of hearing that we call the ears. Similarly, we have the organ of touch, the organ of smell, the organ of taste. Besides these five organs of perception, we have the five organs of action. The organs of perception may be called the sense organs; the organs of action may be called the motor organs. These motor organs are the hands by which we receive or give, the mouth by which we speak, the legs by which we move, the organ of generation, and the organ of evacuation.

In this chapter we are concerned with the five organs of perception and the mind. Each

THE MIND AND THE SENSES

sense organ is responsible for a particular kind of knowledge of the external world, while the mind is responsible for each and every kind of knowledge. Whether you use your perceptual knowledge of the the external world, or your internal perception, or inference, or intuitive knowledge, you have to use your mind. Our knowledge, our happiness, our success in this life depend on the use we make of these important factors of our personality. The senses are our very good friends if we use them rightly; they may turn to be our deadly foes if we fail to use them rightly. One should be very careful how one handles these instruments of knowledge. It is very necessary to know their nature, their functions and their relation to the real Self.

How do these sense organs function? According to the Vedantic view, the eyes and the ears perceive their objects where they are. You see some flowers, and you are actually seeing them there so you know where they are. Similarly, the organ of hearing perceives the sound at a distance. This is why you can know what direction the sound is coming from and whether the sound is very near or far. The organ of touch perceives things when in actual contact; the organ of taste, also, can experience its object only when in actual contact. With the organ of smell it appears that we smell things at a distance. There are the flowers and we can smell them. But do we smell the flowers in actual contact with the nose? Not necessarily, says Vedanta. The object you see, you see at a distance, but the smell you receive is possible only because of the direct contact of the material particles forming the smell with the nose. This is why if you smell something, you do not know exactly where the source of the smell is, but if you hear a sound you know that the sound is coming from a distance, or from nearby, or from a certain direction. You cannot say that about smell.

According to the modern empirical view of knowledge, there is no action at a distance. All sensation is possible only when the object you perceive impinges on your senses. You hear a sound only when the sound vibrations strike, or the minute particles forming the sound vibrations enter your ear and strike the tympanum. Then only can you perceive sound. The streams of matter, however minute they may be, must impinge on your senses. Now, a question arises: if I hear the sound after the sound vibration reaches my eardrum, then how can I say that it is coming from a long distance? Or, suppose you

THE MIND AND THE SENSES

see an object: the light from that object enters your eyes and forms an image on the retina. If the perception happens there, how can you know that the object is standing fifty feet from you? These questions remain unanswered by the modern empirical view of knowledge.

There is another difference between the sense organs. Although every other sense organ has a particular location in this physical body, the organ of touch has no particular location. It is all over the body. However, whatever may be the process of sense perception, each sense organ has a particular function. Here the flowers, the fragrance of the flowers, and the colour and form of the flowers are all closely associated. Your eye will differentiate the form and the colour from the fragrance, but will not receive the fragrance, because it has not the power to receive the fragrance. Similarly, your nose can receive only the fragrance, though you cannot differentiate the fragrance from the colour, but your nose, the particular organ, can differentiate. It has a particular power only for receiving fragrance.

The mind, however, is responsible for all sense perception, being common to all the sense organs. You are seeing a person or hearing his voice. Are the eyes adequate for seeing him, or the ears adequate for hearing his voice? You may be looking at him, your ear may be quite open, still, you may not be able to hear him, or even see him. You were "absent-minded", as the saying goes, and so did not hear or see him. Therefore, the mind is an important factor in every kind of sense perception.

What is this mind? Some say it is a brain function, or a function of the nervous system, or some other bodily activity. Vedanta does not uphold this view. Most of the modern psychologists associate the mind with the body; not only that, they think it is a vital part of the body, or that it is no entity at all. No substance, just a function. If you think the mind is an integral part of the body, how can it be dissociated from your ear or from your eye? If it be a part of the brain—the brain is connected with the tympanum (eardrum)—how can it dissociate itself? If it be an integral part of this body or the nervous system, how can it dissociate itself?

The mind is distinct from the body, according to Vedanta. It is not an integral part of the body and, at the same time, it is not a process or function. There are many mental functions, and we differentiate them from physical activities. For example, our thinking, reasoning, observa-

THE MIND AND THE SENSES

tion, feeling, willing, remembering, and speculating are all classified as mental functions. There are many psychologists who say, yes, these are mental functions, but they are not different from physical activities; they are a certain form of physical action. But if they are explained in terms of physical actions, then we would have been able to observe them. We can observe any mechanical or physical process, but these processes are invisible.

Nobody can use the senses to observe actual thinking, reasoning, willing, desiring, or remembering. The senses establish your contact with the entire external world. If you lose your eyesight, the entire world of form and colour is lost to you. If you lose your hearing, the entire world of sound is lost to you. Your whole contact with this external world, the objective universe that you consider to be so real, is made possible by these senses. When you sleep or you dream, you do not miss this world. It goes out of your consciousness in such a way that you do not miss it.

The mind has the various functions that cannot be explained in terms of mechanical or physical processes because they are not observable by any of the senses. Even so, the mind cannot be considered just a bundle of functions or sensations: the mind is called in Sanskrit *antahkarana*, "internal instrument,". We have external instruments, the sense organs, for external perception. At the same time we perceive two orders of existence: the external, objective order of things, and the internal, subtle order of facts. Just as external perception is a criterion of reality, internal perception also is a criterion of reality.

What makes inner facts real to you? Some kind of perception. What is the instrument of that perception? The mind. Without acknowledging the reality of internal perception, you cannot establish the reality of inner expressions such as love or joy. We cannot perceive them. We perceive their physical expressions by our senses, but not these internal or psychological factors.

We can very clearly distinguish between physical and mental pain. When your heart aches, you know very well whether it is the physical heart or the emotional heart; whether you have to go to a medical doctor or a psychiatrist. How do you clearly distinguish between this physical pain and the mental pain? Because these two things are quite different. They are closely connected, but one is not an integral part of the other. The interaction of the mind and the body has been a very serious problem for psychologists and philosophers, because of a wrong view of the mind. The mind has been allied with the spirit by some; they could not differentiate the mind from the spirit. They thought, because the mind being of the nature of the spirit, it could not be related to this body, which is of the nature of matter. Still, it is a fact that the mind influences the body and the body influences the mind. If you take certain drugs there will be a change in not only your physical system, but also in your mind. How is it possible?

Various explanations have been given for this interaction between the body and the mind. This has been very difficult because they have been conceived to be of contrary nature. Descartes used to give an explanation that he called "parallelism". These two, mind and body, are two distinct principles, but they are synchronized. Two clocks tuned in the same way will always strike at the same time. They simply coordinate—they parallel or synchronize—though there is no actual connection between the two. Then there is the theory called "epiphenomenalism," which says that this mind is just a little light that has come out of the bodily processes, and this light is the passive witness of the physical processes.

Mind has a much more important function. It is dynamic. Truly speaking, mind is not of the nature of spirit, nor is it exactly of the nature of the body. It occupies an intermediate position between the body and the Self. Anything that is not of the nature of spirit, anything that is not self-luminous, anything that has not consciousness as its very essence, that is not aware by nature, that is something other than spirit—that must be classified with matter. From that standpoint mind falls into the category of matter. But it is of a different type of matter than this physical body. It is distinct from the physical body: it is a different principle, it has different functions. Because both mind and body are of a material nature, they can influence one another. Though mind is of a material nature, it can reflect the consciousness of spirit.

Just as physical light is reflected more or less on different objects, similarly, this mind, being made of very refined matter, can reflect the light of the spirit better than this body and the senses. Because of that, mind has a kind of consciousness that is not inherent in the mind—it is the borrowed light of the spirit. A piece of wire if permeated by fire will become aglow. Similarly, the mind becomes aglow with the light of the spirit. The mind, being associated with the eyes, for instance, makes the eyes capable of perceiving external objects. Behind every sense perception there is the principle of cognition: hearing is not a mechanical function, it is a function of cognition; seeing is cognition of a certain object. Every sense function is a form of cognition. The principle of consciousness underlies the senses. That principle of consciousness is transferred to the senses through the mind from the spirit, because true spirit alone has consciousness as its very essence.

The mind has another important function. It stores all the impressions that we receive from our experiences and activities. For example, you see certain things. When you leave the place these will disappear from your vision, but the impressions will still be left within you. The mind receives and stores these impressions. Anything you see, anything you hear, anything you eat, or any action you perform leave their indelible impressions on the mind. Every moment you are gathering such impressions within you. Mind is the storehouse of all the impressions that you have received from your childhood up to the present. Even your thinking leaves an impression; your imagining, your feeling, and every function of the mind also leaves an impression.

These impressions, generally speaking, may be classified under good and evil impressions, under high and low impressions, under right and wrong impressions. If we have right impressions, these elevate our quality of life. If we have wrong impressions, they lower our quality of life. They are the source of our likes and dislikes, and they become the origin of our memory. They form our disposition, our character; these impressions form our entire future life. The impressions fructify in course of time and bring us joy or misery, light or darkness, bondage or freedom. So one has to be very careful how the senses and the mind are used. The effect of perception does not end the moment the object of perception is gone. If you do an evil deed, it leaves an indelible impression on the mind.

The impressions dwell within the mind in two different ways. They may be manifest within the mind, or they may be unmanifest. Hindu psychology does not divide the mind into watertight compartments as conscious or uncon-

THE MIND AND THE SENSES 93

scious. Any part of the mind may be conscious; any part of the mind may be subconscious or unconscious. What is the conscious mind? It is that part of the mind which comes within the vision of ego-consciousness. If you extend the purview of this ego-consciousness you can have more of the mind within your vision. The part of the mind that is beyond the range of this ego-consciousness may be called the subconscious mind.

The impressions that are in the subconscious mind dwell there in different states. The first state is the overpowered state. These impressions are not weak, or dead, or asleep: they are overpowered. An enemy that is overpowered can still hurt you. The overpowered impressions are always struggling to do something. Our good tendencies are overpowered when certain evil associations prevail around us. Our evil tendencies are overpowered when we live in good associations. Some calamity happens and certain wrong tendencies become suppressed or overpowered for a time. Bad impressions have to be gradually weakened by constant counter efforts. That is the purpose of education and cultural development. But as long as these wrong impressions are there, your life is not quite safe. By right associations, by thinking good thoughts, by doing good deeds, a person should constantly try to reshape these wrong tendencies.

Neither the senses nor the mind is the actual perceiver. The real perceiver is beyond the senses and the mind. Do the eyes see? Do the ears hear? Does the mouth speak? Or is it someone who sees through the eyes, hears through the ears, and speaks through the mouth? The same one functions through all these organs and the mind. That which is common to all must be distinct from all: it cannot be an inherent part of any of these. The real experiencer, the perceiver, is distinct from all the senses and the mind.

If a person loses his eyesight after seeing something, he can still remember it. If the eyes saw the thing and also received the impression, memory would not have been possible after the loss of eyesight. For instance, a person saw the Himalaya mountains, then twenty years later he lost his eyesight. He can still recall the picture of the Himalaya mountains. What is it that recalls the picture of the Himalayas? It is the same thing that was responsible for seeing the Himalayas twenty years before. If the eyes are not the actual perceiver, it must be the mind. But it cannot be mind which is the perceiver, because the mind

THE MIND AND THE SENSES

itself is perceived. Just as external objects fall into the category of the observed, so do your mental fear, or joy, or love, or hatred. Why can you observe the functions of the mind? Because you are distinct from the mind. You can see the functions of your mind because the mind is not the seer. The real you is the seer.

These senses, apart from being the instruments of knowledge, are also the instruments of pleasure. They bring us great pleasure; we are very anxious to have that pleasure. The senses have a tendency to objectify things and derive pleasure. The human mind, or the human spirit in association with the mind and the senses, is always seeking pleasure from external objects. This craving of the senses is without limit. The more you get, the more you want. The senses are ever hungry for sense enjoyment. In this way the senses delude us. We think that what is pleasant is also invariably good—but it is not so. What is pleasant is not necessarily good. This is a fact that we often forget.

In judging the activities of the senses we should know that the senses provide us with pleasures and we want these pleasures, but these pleasures are not always good. Sense enjoyment does not necessarily ensure health, or real happiness, or strength, or wisdom. Sometimes these experiences tire you too much, and blur your vision. Why? Because sense pleasures are not the highest avocations of man. Greater than this sense pleasure is intellectual delight. People who taste intellectual delight lose interest in the sense pleasures. Greater than this intellectual delight is the joy that comes from moral purity. And greater than moral purity is the light of the spirit, because spiritual development alone leads to complete self-fulfilment. It removes all darkness from within and removes all bondage forever.

In order to gain the true objective of life, we have to direct the senses and the mind from the level of sense pleasure to the intellectual level, from that level to the moral level, and from that level to the spiritual level. Self-control does not mean that you are to torture the senses and the mind, or that you should repress or suppress them. You are to direct their course from the lower to the higher level. In order to do that you must establish your mastery over them. You simply recognize yourself as the master; these eyes, for instance, are your instruments, and they have to serve you. Even this mind, however important it may be, is to serve you. You are the master: assert your mastery. The real spirit is ever pure, ever luminous, shining and immortal, but, being identified with the instrument, you think you are mortal. There is no impurity in pure spirit; you become impure being associated with the impure mind and body. Whatever defect there may be in you is due to the defect or deficiency of the senses and the mind. In pure spirit there is no deficiency. Why do the senses and the mind become deficient? Because you fail to use them rightly. Instead of directing them towards the higher goal, you allow them to gravitate to the lower level.

Not only do you rise to the next higher stage by controlling the mind and the senses, you can reach the highest goal just by the right use of the mind and the senses. You can reach the Supreme Goal where there is complete self-fulfilment. When this is attained there remains nothing more to seek: this is the removal of all darkness, all misery, all bondage; this is where you enter into life that has no end, and where joy is limitless. ❑

6. THE MIND AND ITS CONTROL

Controlling the mind is a universal human problem, except for those blessed few who rise above the human level by realizing their innate divinity. About five thousand years ago, Arjuna approached Sri Krishna with the same problem of control of the mind. In the Bhagavad-Gita, Arjuna says to Sri Krishna: "Verily, the mind, O Krishna, is restless, turbulent, strong, and unyielding; I regard it quite as hard to achieve its control as that of the wind." Sri Krishna replied: "Without doubt, O mighty-armed, the mind is restless and difficult to control; but through practise and renunciation, it may be controlled" (chapter 6, verses 34, 35). By detaching the mind from all that is temporal, through persistent effort, and fixing the mind upon the Supreme Being, control of the mind is achieved.

Of course, this instruction is given with regard to spiritual aspirants who have realized the

THE MIND AND ITS CONTROL

futility of all search for the temporal and whose sole purpose in life is to realize the Supreme Being, the One that is eternal. But this instruction may also apply to everyone. Whoever is willing to practise self-control can benefit from it. The principle is this: You have to make a point of daily practice to fix the mind on the higher. That is the sole secret of self-control. Anything that you accept as an ideal, hold to it and do not let the mind be diverted to a lower level.

Anyone who wants to live properly should know what he lives for. He should seek something noble in this life, even though the mind may still have a tendency to move toward the lower levels. To overcome this tendency, he must practise control of the entire physical body, the organs, and the mind, to direct them to the higher ideal. That is the whole secret of self-control. The term *self-control* means actually the control of the psychophysical system by the real Self—the control of the lower self by the higher Self.

To understand this, we should know what the position of the mind is in the human system. Is it all-important? Is it supreme? What place does it occupy? The mind is distinct on the one hand from this physical body and the organs located within it, and on the other hand, it is distinct from the real Self. It occupies an intermediary position between the real Self and the body.

In Western thought, the mind is often confused with the real Self; but the real Self is actually the knower within. This knower within cognizes the external objects through the five organs of perception: it sees through the eyes various forms and colours, hears through the ears various sounds, tastes through the palate, smells through the nostrils, feels hard or soft things with the organ of touch. That cognizer of the external objects is the Self, the real man. Each organ has a specific function—the eyes can only see, the ears can only hear—still we say *I* hear, *I* see. There is something common to all the organs: the Knower, which must be distinct from all of them. That Knower is the real Self, who not only hears and sees things, but also thinks, feels, imagines, remembers, and so forth.

Self-control means the power to distinguish the real Self from the not-self, to distinguish this knowing Self, the knower, from all that is known. We identify ourselves with the sense organs, so we become controlled by the sense organs. We identify with the mind, so we become submerged in the mental waves of the mind. Vedanta says that you have to know what you are and assert yourself as you really are. When you distinguish yourself from this not-self, the psychophysical organism, you will be able to control the body, the mind, and the organs. Very few develop the power of reasoning by which they can discriminate the real Self from the not-self; however, we shall follow the steps by which a person can rise to this stage.

According to Vedanta, the mind has the functions (that psychologists recognize) of cognition, volition, and emotion. Of these, cognition is primary because you cannot feel anything unless you have knowledge of that thing. Cognition has a fourfold function: deliberation, determination, egoism, and recollection. Deliberation leaves us in doubt, hesitating, wavering: you see something, but you cannot ascertain what it is. Then you refer to some previous experience and you say, "Yes, I have seen that before," and you know what it is. This is determination. This power of determination is very important, according to Vedanta. You must come to a decision with regard to a thing before your volition can function rightly, before you can succeed in controlling the emotions. Determination implies the power of reason, the power to distinguish between the apparent and the false, between the pleasant and the good, between right and wrong. Only then, can you come to the conclusion, "Yes, this is right, this course should be followed." Then volition will obey. This *buddhi*, determination, comes to a decisive point through reasoning, then will follows. These two, determination and will, are very important in cultivating the self.

Cultivating the self, actually the cultivation of human life, means the cultivation of the mind. Development of the human individual means the development of the mind. Your intellectual development, your aesthetic development, your moral development, your spiritual development, all mean the development of your mind. Mind is the most important instrument in the human personality. All development depends on the mind. Your success and failure, your pain and pleasure, your strength and weakness, your knowledge and ignorance, your virtue and vice, all depend on the mind. So the mind is very, very important.

In order to control the mind, before you exercise the power of discrimination between the Self and the not-self, you must develop the

THE MIND AND ITS CONTROL

power of determination. Through reasoning you come to a decision, then your volition will function, and you will be able to control your emotions. If you are in a stage of doubt or hesitancy, you cannot pursue a course with your will, and you cannot control your emotions. You must come to a determination as to what you should do, and then volition will obey your determination. Reason plus volition can control the emotions. Desires and emotions are not bad in themselves, they just have to be given right direction. As long as you have desires for sense enjoyment, they may lead you astray. But you can turn these desires to higher ideals, to higher goals.

For those who do not desire anything temporal, but desire the realization of God, this is not called desire because wanting God realization means you are not seeking anything external. You are trying to be established in what you really are; that is, you are trying to be established in your relationship with divinity, in your innate purity and blissfulness.

Desires themselves are not discarded, they are turned higher. Emotion is also like this. For example, instead of being angry with others' failings, be angry with your own. Instead of being proud of the things of this world, be proud of your given heritage. You are a child of the Supreme Lord. You are supposed to walk in the path of light and truth. In this way, even pride and anger are not discarded, but are used to advance on the spiritual path.

In Vedantic tradition there is a story of a blind man who could walk, and a lame man who could see. They pooled their resources and the lame man climbed on the shoulders of the blind man. Then the lame man who could see directed the blind man who could walk to where they wanted to go. So the two men worked in harmony and they got along very well. Similarly, our reason and our emotion together can be very well harmonized under the guidance of reason. Vedanta has very much stressed the power of reason, leading to determination and control of the will by the power of right decision.

The question arises as to how this power of determination can be developed. Until the mind is purified to a great extent, the power of reasoning does not exist. Now, how does one purify the mind if purification of the mind means clearing the mind, of all undesirable emotions such as anger, jealousy, hatred, malice, fear, lust, and greed? You may say that if you have the power of discrimination, then will and reason together can control the emotions. But, before the powers of reasoning and will are developed, your emotions lead you astray. This is the problem of human life.

Vedanta says that a child develops his emotional nature long before he develops his power of reason and power of volition. Before he knows the distinction between pleasant and good, he is drawn by what is pleasant. Some delicious food comes to him, and he will gulp it down even though he does not know whether the food will be good for him. It is delicious, that is enough. He sees a person or some beautiful sight, and he welcomes it because it is pleasant, therefore, it must be good. Unfortunately, the pleasant often appears as though it were good, and that is a tragedy of life. Pleasant and good become mixed up. The great battle a person has to fight in this life is to separate the attractive from the really good.

In the early years, children must be under the guidance of their elders. If you permit them to do whatever they like, you will ruin them. They will come under the grip of lust and greed, and money will become everything to them. "Enjoy whatever is pleasant," will become their watchword. It is the duty of parents, teachers, and other elders to teach them by example and precept what is the right way. Make them understand what is truth, and gradually they will follow the right path of self-control and not permit their minds to be swayed by anger, jealousy, hatred or lust.

When the human mind is attached to anything temporal, it is subject to all the emotions. If your mind is attracted to one individual, all other emotions will be associated with that person for fear of losing him. If others become drawn to the same person, somehow, you will become jealous. If you can win that person, somehow, you will become proud of your victory. From this one attachment has come fear, pride, jealousy, and many other emotions. If you are subject to mental problems it is due to lack of proper training at an early age.

It is the duty of adults to control the younger generation until they develop the power of discrimination. If early training is not given, lust and greed will take hold of the young minds. If the person is well guided by precepts and examples at an early age, if he can learn some self-control from others, then he will develop the powers of understanding and of right judgement and will. Then he will be able to control his own emotions. Until a person develops right understanding, moral life does not come naturally. But when he develops right understanding and can control his emotions, then he becomes moral on his own initiative. Until then his moral life must be compulsory.

If you do not guide children along the moral path from the very beginning, they will eventually be guided by the state laws. If your family laws are not upheld, the government laws, the policemen and the military powers will control your children. Let them be disciplined at an early age so they will grow in the power of understanding, and they will take care of themselves.

Those who can accept the spiritual ideals through the development of their will power should do some spiritual exercise every day. They should try to direct their body, their organs, their minds, their thoughts, their deeds, and their words toward the achievement of the Goal Supreme. Those who cannot accept this spiritual ideal should accept at least some noble goal in life. Eating, drinking, sleeping, and some sense enjoyment are what human beings have in common with all the lower animals. The human being is capable of much more. Man can cultivate his mind, and, along with it, aesthetic, moral and spiritual power. Every individual needs some noble ideal to follow. If he has no ideal to follow, he cannot discipline himself truly.

The secret of control of the mind is this: What do you live for? Ask this question of yourself. Unless you find a satisfactory answer to this question, you cannot have peace of mind. Find something worthwhile to live for, and direct yourself completely toward the achievement of that goal. That is *tapas*. In a commentary Sankaracharya says that tapas means this: directing your entire psychophysical being to the achievement of a goal. If you can choose the spiritual ideal, the realization of God, as the highest goal, well and good. But if you cannot choose that, you must find some worthy ideal to live for. Without that you cannot have real peace of mind. When you have found that worthy ideal to live for, then you should direct all your energy to the attainment of that goal. You should associate with persons who will help you reach your goal. If, for instance, you have an ambition to be a literary person, you should practise writing every day. That will check your sense desires quite well. So the secret of self-control is the choosing of a noble ideal and withdrawing the mind as far as possible from the lower to the higher.

It is true that the mind is very restless, turbulent, stubborn, but remember that this restlessness is not innate in the mind. Mind is, truly speaking, made of pure substance. Serenity is an innate characteristic of the mind. It wants to be serene, calm; yet it is restless because there are extraneous factors that throw it out of balance. Like a placid lake, it becomes disturbed when you throw a rock into it. That rock is an extraneous factor. In the case of the mind the disturbing factors come from our own actions and thoughts.

Whatever we experience, whatever we do, whatever thoughts we think leave an impression on the mind; these impressions do not always dwell on the surface. They go to the bottom, then dwell in the subconscious mind. They are not perceivable by the ego because they go below the range of ego consciousness. That part of the mind within the range of ego consciousness is the conscious mind, but many of the impressions of our experiences and thoughts lie deep in the subconscious level. These subconscious urges influence our conscious mind, and therefore they must be controlled. We cannot directly deal with subconscious urges or tendencies or desires until they surface in the conscious mind and we become aware of them. But they can be controlled by controlling our activities in daily life, and by our thoughts in the waking state.

There are wrong tendencies and desires within a person, so how can he control them? They will come to the surface of the mind sometimes and disturb him. For this reason he should try to rectify his conscious life as far as possible. The fight with the subconscious mind must be fought in the conscious mind. You cannot reach the subconscious mind directly, no matter what may be there. If there are wrong tendencies within, you overcome them by contrary tendencies. If, for instance, there is a tendency toward violence within, by cultivating contrary tendencies such as kindness and forgiveness, you overcome the violent tendency. This is the method which Patanjali has hinted at in his Yoga Sutras.

The mind is made of pure substance. Because it is made of pure substance, it is the transmitter of consciousness. Consciousness belongs to the real Self. The mind looks as if it has consciousness in itself, but it actually does not. It becomes aglow with the radiance of the Self, just

THE MIND AND ITS CONTROL

as an iron ball, if well heated, becomes aglow, or just as glass permeated by light appears effulgent. Similarly, this mind, because it is made of pure substance, serves as the transmitter of consciousness which belongs to the Self.

The mind transmits consciousness to the physical body. Unless the mind transmits consciousness, the eyes cannot see. You are looking at me but you don't see me because the mind is distracted. Just the eyes cannot see, just the ears cannot hear, just the mouth cannot speak, just the hands cannot work—the mind must be associated with each of the organs, the motor organs as well as the sense organs. The mind must bring the light of consciousness to this physical body, then the organs and the body can function. This is why the mind is the greatest instrument of knowledge and action. It is through the concentration of the mind that you gain knowledge. Unless you can concentrate the mind you cannot know anything.

We have to practise control of the mind to attain knowledge in anything. This mind, because it is made of pure substance, can transmit consciousness. It is pure substance, its very nature is pure. Extraneous things that have gathered in the subconscious and conscious mind cause disturbances. The first thing is to rectify them by the exercise of reason, to clear the mind of the wrong and let the right remain. This has to be done in the waking state. Through the exercise of reason you will gradually be able to develop real understanding, and learn to discriminate between the Self and the not-self.

As stated before, the first thing necessary is to find an ideal, a great ideal in life that you can hold to and devote yourself whole-heartedly to its attainment. This is the great secret of self-control. It will lead to the power of discrimination between the Self and the not-self. The power of discrimination will develop your will power, and that will enable you to control the emotions also. Both emotion and reason are necessary, but the emotions must be controlled by will. ❑

7. WAKING, DREAMING, AND DEEP SLEEP

Every human being experiences daily the three states of waking, dreaming, and deep sleep, but not many know what these experiences actually mean. By careful analysis of these experiences we can know the real nature of a human being. The experiences change, but the experiencer is constant; so a person can say: "I wake, I dream, I sleep." This constant experiencer, the knowing Self within, is the very centre of the human personality, and it is at the same time self-shining. It has consciousness as its very essence. This is the fundamental difference between the experiencer and the experienced, the knower and the known. The knower has consciousness as its very essence; the known is devoid of consciousness. The known falls into the category of material existence. The knower is considered to be spiritual existence, that is, something that is characterized by self-awareness.

A light bulb is evidently self-manifest, but it has no self-awareness. But the light of consciousness, which is the very nature of the spiritual Self, is self-luminous and self-aware. This spiritual self—the one constant factor in human personality—the experiencer of the waking state, of the dream state, and of the sleep state, is characterized by awareness. It is not only luminous, but it is self-luminous. Being self-luminous it is very pure and ever bright, that is, there is no trace of darkness in it. By studying these three states—wake, dream, and deep sleep—we find that man has an inner being that is pure, shining, changeless, and constant.

What is the waking state? In the waking state this physical body plays its full part. This physical body establishes the contact of the inner Self with the outside world and is the medium of waking experience; therefore, consciousness is very closely associated with this physical body in the waking state. All the different organs are operative. The five organs of perception are active, ever ready to cognize this objective universe. In addition, the five organs of action are also ready to operate. Because a person identifies himself with the physical body in the waking state, so his ego is based on the consciousness of

WAKING, DREAMING...

the physical body. A person realizes, "I am so-and-so, I weigh so much, I am dark or fair, I am a man or a woman, I belong to such and such family, I was born in such and such a country, I hold such and such a position." All these ego ideas have their basis in the consciousness of this physical body, or the identification of the Self with this physical body. So, during waking state a person has a very clear, definite ego-idea rooted in this physical body, and he always tries to assert this ego-idea by all possible means.

When he dreams, his consciousness recedes from this physical body. Naturally, the body cannot function in the way it was functioning. In the waking state, because of this pronounced ego-idea, a person has definite *will*. He has self-determination; he has also some standards of judgment that he always tries to maintain, some idea of propriety. But when he dreams, his consciousness recedes from the physical body, and as soon as consciousness recedes, contact is lost with the whole external universe. He is no longer aware of what is happening in this universe. In deep sleep state he does not miss even his dearest child. The physical body, even the brain, is inoperative. Only certain automatic functions of the body continue: some digestive processes, circulation of blood through the beating of the heart. Otherwise, the physical body is almost inoperative.

In the dream state, the body is active to a very small extent, but the mind is very active. The mind is part of what is called the *subtle body*. Just as this physical body is the chief medium, or seat of waking experience, similarly, the subtle body is composed primarily of the five organs of action, the five organs of perception, and the mind. The external organs of perception and organs of action are not the real organs: their subtle counterparts are real.

The subtle body is the storehouse of all the impressions that we gather during our waking hours. Whatever we perceive by these external organs of perception leaves an impression on the mind. Whatever we do by these organs of action also leaves an impression on the mind. We are constantly accumulating impressions upon the mind. The subtle body, the principal factor of which is the mind, is painted with these impressions, which are very potent. They create our tendencies, our habits; they create our likes and dislikes; they also live within us as the seed forces that create a new situation for reaping the fruits of our deeds and experiences.

WAKING, DREAMING...

During the dream state, the mind becomes free from the body idea. It becomes associated with any impression that may be prevalent in the mind. When it is dominated by that impression, the mind has a particular ego idea. A dreamer can have any kind of ego. A queen may think she is a beggar-woman. Any kind of ego can exist there, because you do not know which impression will be prevalent in a person while dreaming. The will and power of judgment that are associated with the ego idea based upon the physical body, does not exist anymore. Therefore, we do not have any kind of self-determination or definite *will* in the dream state. We do not have even any definite judgment or consistency or propriety in dream. In dream state, a person does not have a definite ego idea. One does not have any definite standard of judgment, so nothing seems incoherent in a dream. One also lacks in will power, and one cannot resist when resistance is necessary. Any tendency, desire, or idea may be prevalent at that time. We are actually at the mercy of the tendency or desire that prevails at that time. Being influenced by that desire, or will, or wish, the mind creates an image or picture out of those impressions. The impressions become concretized. Just as we can see a picture painted on a canvas in all three dimensions, similarly, this mind is like a piece of canvas painted by all these impressions gathered during waking hours.

During sleep a person may have some desire which becomes the cause of a dream. According to some modern psychologists, particularly the school of Freud, dream experience is created by repressed desires and tendencies. This does not give a complete idea of dreams. Dreams are created, no doubt, by suppressed desires and tendencies, but, in addition, there are many other sources of dreams. Dreams, it is true, are the compensation of our unfulfilled desires; the mind compensates itself during dreams. For example, a person tried to make a fortune, but could not reach his goal. Still, the desire was in his mind. He dreams that he has found a source of hoarded wealth, and, all of a sudden, he becomes immensely rich. By this dream, his unfulfilled desire is compensated. Fear and hope may also create a dream. A person suffering from an incurable illness dreams that he was completely cured, but when he wakes nothing had been changed.

Dreams are caused, Shankara points out, by desires and tendencies. Behind these desires and tendencies are the impressions stored in the mind. They are the material for dream imagery. A person may also have some prophetic vision in a dream. Some spiritual problems have been solved in dreams. Even mathematical problems and scientific problems have been solved in dreams. A person may be raised to a very high spiritual level in a dream. It is true that these impressions are stored in the subconscious and are certainly not all bad. There are also very good impressions, and when those impressions prevail, a person may have a very wonderful spiritual dream.

One person was very much dejected and he could not find solace anywhere in this world. One day he dreamed that a certain holy person, a great spiritual leader for whom he had very much admiration, appeared to him. He at once fell down at his feet, and the holy man, that spiritual leader, placed his hand on his head. All his fears were chased away, and he had from that dream some strength which sustained him throughout the rest of his life. This is a fact, and this has happened not only to one person. I, myself, have known several persons who have had such an experience.

In the dream state, sometimes, spiritual experiences come in symbolic forms. I recall one incident that I cannot forget. When I was in Benares in 1921 living at the feet of Swami Turiyananda, one of the direct disciples of Sri Ramakrishna, we used to meet every day in his room. One of the swamis said: "Last night I had a very wonderful dream. I had some doubt about a spiritual fact. There are great spiritual leaders of the rank of Christ, or Buddha, or Sri Krishna, or Sankara, who are considered even as saviours of human souls; and there are also great saints and sages. I did not know exactly whether these great saviours were in any way fundamentally different from these saints and sages. This was my doubt: When a person obtains complete illumination, can he not be ranked with those whom we call saviours? I saw in my dream such great spiritual leaders as Christ, Sri Krishna, and Buddha, ranged on one side and the great spiritual personalities, sages whom the world worships as free souls, ranged on another side. Then they all walked upon the waves—this all happened on a sea beach. The seers and saints walked some distance then they came back, but the great spiritual leaders whom we call saviours walked very, very far, out of sight before they came back again to the shore."

This dream illustrated the great difference of spiritual power between these two classes of spiritual leaders, the saints and sages on one hand, and the saviours on the other. The saviours have tremendous power; they not only save themselves and those who are closely connected with them for years and years, but for centuries, they form the bridge between this mortal life and the immortal spirituality. They are like huge steamboats that can carry thousands of passengers. These great saviours form a class by themselves. They are not just bound souls who have attained complete illumination or freedom. This truth was symbolized in concrete form in the dream mentioned above. So dreams have many different causes, not just one particular cause. From this dream state, a person passes into the deep sleep state.

In deep sleep a person loses what we call consciousness. In the dream state the mind is active, creating many images. You have some ego-ideas, although they are not very definite. But when you enter into deep sleep, you no longer have any mental functions, no thought, no idea, no feeling, no imagination, no memory of any kind. All the variations of the mind are completely hushed; all your fears and worries subside. There is a state of complete darkness in the mind, unspecified ignorance. You do not know anything. In the waking state you have specified ignorance, you know that you do not know this or that. But in deep sleep you have no knowledge, and even your ignorance is unspecified. You know nothing. All the features of the mind enter into a state of homogeneity covered by unspecified darkness; even this ego-consciousness does not prevail anymore. A mother, as the Upanishad says, does not know she is a mother. The father does not know he is a father, a queen does not know she is a queen, a beggar does not know he is a beggar. This ego-consciousness drops altogether. What happens then? You are completely relaxed. You enter into a state of complete naturalness, free from all cares and worries. Every day, during the twent-four hours, you have to get rid of this ego-idea in order to have complete rest. Then, when you get up, this ego-idea again works upon you, and cares and worries and the sense of responsibilities come.

You have to get rid of this ego-idea based on body-consciousness every day in order to get rest, because this ego-idea is something imposed upon you. You constantly think that you are a physical body, and so you assert this ego-idea in

WAKING, DREAMING...

every possible way. That ego-idea is the cause of your bondage; it is the cause of your pain and also pleasure—both go together. It is the cause of your birth and it is the cause of your death. It is the cause of your youth and it is the cause of your old age. You must nullify this ego-idea every day in order to get rest, to be free of all cares and worries. If you do not do that, you will go crazy.

In the dream state you do not have full rest, because some kind of ego-idea is imposed on the real Self. Waking has its variation: ceaseless change characterizes this waking experience. Similarly, dream state has its variation—ceaseless change. Is there any change in the sleep experience in which you experience unspecified ignorance, a state of complete homogeneity of the mind? Yes, in deep sleep also there is a little variety, as noted by Patanjali, the great Hindu philosopher and psychologist, and the founder of Raja Yoga. He says that sleep experience also varies. A person wakes from deep sleep, and still, he does not feel completely rested. He did not have any actual dream, but he doesn't feel completely rested. Some days he feels completely rested and other days not.

Patanjali says that in deep sleep state, *tamas* prevails. Tamas is one of the three factors that compose the causal body. The homogeneous state of the mind in deep sleep is called the *causal body*. Just as in the seed all the different features of the tree are latent, similarly, there is a causal state in which all the features of the mind are latent. That state of the mind is called the causal body. Just as this physical body is the chief medium of waking experience, and the subtle body is the chief medium of the dream experience, the causal body is the chief medium of the sleep experience.

This causal body is composed of three factors: *sattva*, *rajas*, and *tamas*. Tamas is sometimes associated with sattva. When it is associated with sattva a person experiences very good, peaceful sleep. When tamas is associated with rajas, then he does not feel that kind of peace. He feels some kind of uneasiness after sleep and the body is not quite ready to work. When tamas is very much predominant, overpowering rajas and sattva completely, then a person, even after sleep, feels very indolent. So, even in deep sleep there is a variation of experience. Deep sleep is not a state of complete unconsciousness. This is why you can say, I slept peacefully, I did not know anything.

Throughout these ever-changing experiences, there is one abiding self. There have been

WAKING, DREAMING...

psychologists who have tried to prove that there is no enduring self, or that the self is constantly changing. If the self changes, then the fact of knowledge and memory cannot be explained. There is a continuity underlying all these varying experiences, and that is the real self of each and every individual. That self is immortal; that self is self-existent. If you analyse the waking, dreaming, and deep sleep states, you find that there is a self underlying all these experiences. The waking experiences pass, the dream experiences pass, the sleep experiences pass, but that self remains unrelated to these states. The spiritual self, which is not connected with this body, which is not intrinsically connected even with the mind, that real self, the witness, the observer of even the sleep state, that is always there. It is *That* which actually sees through the eyes, hears through the ears, works through the hands. You forget your very self and identify yourself with that which you are not; that is the cause of all your bondage and suffering.

These three experiences Vedanta has analysed in order to discover the real nature of a human being. The conclusion is this: Your real self is untarnished by all these changing conditions. Everything in this world changes, but there is one thing that is constant in you, and that constant factor is the real *you*. This is ever shining, pure, free, immortal, self-existent, because you never doubt your existence; you have to presuppose your existence. There must be a doubter in order to doubt. That self, which is self-revealing, which you cannot doubt even, that self is the real Being of each and every individual. That self is the manifestation of the Supreme Being. That spiritual self is the Supreme Self dwelling in the psychophysical system. By realizing that spiritual self you realize the Supreme Being. You contact Spirit through spirit. You reach the soul of the universe by reaching that very Soul. So the Upanishads say again and again: Inside this inner zone, the golden case of consciousness, there is the spiritual self, ever shining, pure and free, unrelated , ever the witness of all these changing conditions that you experience in the waking state, in dream state, and in deep sleep state. Meditate on the self. That self is not confined within this psychophysical system, that self is actually one with the Supreme Self. You will find the Truth, the Reality, the Ideal that you conceive as God. That Supreme Being you find just by realizing this very self, and that self is ever the Knower,

WAKING, DREAMING...

never the known. How can you know the Ultimate Knower? That self is ever the Seer and never the seen; that self is ever the Hearer and never the heard; that self is ever the Thinker and never the thought. It is behind all thoughts. The Ultimate Reality is behind everything. There is no knower of That which is the Ultimate Knower.

Sankara points out the nature of the self after analysing waking, dreaming and deep sleep:

Now I shall tell you the nature of the *Atman* (Sanskrit for this true self). If you realize it, you will be freed from the bonds of ignorance and attain liberation. There is a self-existent Reality which is the basis of our consciousness of ego. That Reality is the witness of the three states of consciousness—waking, dreaming, and deep sleep—and is distinct from the five bodily coverings. That Reality is the knower in all states of consciousness, waking, dream, and deep sleep; it is aware of the presence or absence of the mind and its functions. It is the Atman. It also knows that waking passes and dream comes, dream passes, sleep comes. Even in the interval it exists. The cessation of dream and the presence of sleep, the cessation of waking and the presence of dream, that also it records.

Vivekachudamani, 124-126

That Reality sees everything by its own light. We see everything apparently through the light of the sun, or an artificial light. Actually it is through the light of the self that we see everything. Do you think that a physical light manifests these things to you? If you sleep, or become absent-minded, does this physical light manifest anything to you?

The actual light is in the pure spiritual self, which is self-aware; this physical light, however resplendent it may be, is not self-aware. It has no awareness of itself or anything else. Now this light that is characterized by awareness is the pure spirit within, the spiritual Self. That spiritual self has its own light and that light comes through the mind, through the eyes; and that light of consciousness coming through the mind and the eyes illuminates this light. This light illuminated by the light of consciousness reveals all things to you. When in darkness you walk with a lantern in your hand, the light of the lantern first falls upon the different objects, illuminating them, then you see the objects. Similarly, in the waking state, your consciousness moves through

WAKING, DREAMING...

the mind and through the eyes to fall upon everything. Physical light only helps you when it is illuminated by your own consciousness. When it is illuminated by your own consciousness, it has the power to reveal things to you. Behind this physical light is the light of your own spiritual self. Otherwise, why does not this physical light reveal things to this chair; why does it not reveal things to a sleeping man? There are persons who sleep with their eyes open. Do they see things? Can the sun manifest anything to them? The sun has the power to reveal things as long as the sun is illuminated by the light of consciousness. Behind all light, there is the light of consciousness which is considered to be the Light of all lights.

That Reality sees everything by its own light, no one sees it. It gives intelligence to the mind and the intellect, and no one gives it light. That reality pervades the universe, but no one penetrates it. It alone shines. The universe shines with its reflected light. Because of its presence, the body, senses, mind and intellect apply themselves to their respective functions as though obeying its command. Its nature is eternal consciousness. It knows all things from the sense of ego to the body itself. It is the knower of pleasure and pain and of the sense objects. It knows everything objectively, just as a man knows the objective existence of a jar. This is the Atman, the Supreme Being, the ancient, ever new (ever old, ever new, because ever the same). It never ceases to experience infinite joy. It is always the same. It is consciousness itself. The organs and vital energies function under Its command. Here, within this body and the pure mind, in the secret chamber of intelligence, in the infinite universe within the heart, the Atman shines in its captivating splendour like a noon day sun. By its light the universe is revealed. ❏

8. SAMADHI OR SUPERCONSCIOUS EXPERIENCE

There is an experience called *samadhi*, or transcendental experience, which is not easy to attain. Rare individuals attain it after long preparation. This is the only kind of experience that makes a man free from all bondage, that satisfies completely man's deep longing for eternal life, for complete peace and blessedness. None of the three everyday experiences can give us this freedom. These states, waking, dreaming, or deep sleep, are completely incapable of freeing a man from the bondage of life, or of enabling a man to conquer death.

Man is very proud of this waking experience. Whatever he achieves, whatever he knows, is in the waking state. In this waking state he is fully conscious of this external world, and more or less conscious of his relationship to it. His mind functions, his volition and reason are active in the waking state. His five sense organs are active: he can hear, he can see, he can taste things, he can smell things, he can touch things. Just as the organs of perception are all active, the organs of action are also functioning. He can grasp things with the hands, he can walk about, he can talk, and so forth. Whatever man has achieved in the field of science, or philosophy, or in the field of art, or in any other sphere of human activity, has been achieved through the exercise of volition and reasoning power in the waking state. In the dream state, volition does not function. There is no voluntary function during the dream state, nor is there any voluntary function in sleep. But even in the waking state, man, with all his pretensions to scientific achievement and philosophical knowledge, cannot go beyond the common drama of life: he cannot overcome this play of birth, growth, decay, and death.

After birth there will be growth, and after growth there will be decay, and then death. This is something common to every individual life that no human knowledge, no exploration in space, has been able to change. In that common background of life with all its achievements, this life continues to be a drama of smile and tears, of love and hatred, of success and failure, of honour and dishonour. This is the drama that continues to be enacted from one end of the world to another, from primitive time to the modern age. So far as the common background of life is concerned, human knowledge has not gone very far, because achievement in the waking state is not meant for that. Sense perception cannot reveal to you the truth behind this sense world. Yet, it is on the truth behind the sense world that the religious strivings of man are based. It is on the reality beyond this sense world that ethical idealism is based. It is on the reality beyond this sense world that metaphysical conceptions are based. Yet your reason cannot take us to that realm. Until we reach that realm, until we know the Truth, we cannot be free.

What is the way? "Know the Truth and the Truth will make you free." Until you know that Truth you cannot be free. Some may say: "Well, give up the effort, it is impossible to attain. Just continue to be satisfied with this world where you are continuously trying to gain security in the insecure." Is that all of life? Some will say: "Yes, you make hay while the sun shines. Try to squeeze as much juice as you can from these dry bones of life." Many psychologists, many philosophers, many scientists will tell you this is all there is. But the human mind refuses to believe this: "No, I am not meant for death. I am not meant for this drama of love and hatred, of pleasure and pain. Deep within my heart there is a cry for complete freedom from all bondage. Can that be satisfied?" No philosopher or scientist can say. But there have been mystics in the world who have declared in an unequivocal voice that there is a way to attain that Truth; there is a way to conquer death; there is a way to attain peace that passeth understanding, the peace that this world cannot give you.

Down through the ages a message comes from one of the Vedic seers: "Hear me, oh children of immortal bliss, all that dwell in the higher spheres, all that dwell in this world, hear me. I have gone beyond all darkness, I have realized the Supreme Being resplendent as the sun, self-luminous consciousness, beyond all darkness, and by knowing That alone a person goes beyond all darkness, beyond all death. There is no other way to immortality." Just as our waking experience, dream experience, and sleep experience are facts, similarly, there is transcendental experience of the Supreme Reality, beyond sense perception, beyond even intellectual comprehension. How can man attain that? The Upanishads say it comes through deep meditation. But it does require some preparation.

The mind should be purified and the understanding made clear, then that deep meditation will be possible. It is declared by one of the Upanishads that, aided or unaided, the eyes cannot see That. Speech cannot express That. It is beyond all limitation because expression means definition and that means limitation. Mind fails to comprehend That, which is beyond the range of the mind. The hands cannot grasp That. Yet that Supreme Reality, self-effulgent, can be realized through deep meditation when the mind is purified. How? Through the purification of the understanding. A person should have a clear idea of the limitations of the world and life as it is. It is true that in order to live in this world we need good health, we need wealth, we need friends, we need a good home, we need many other things, but none of these actually can give us the kind of satisfaction or freedom we want. None of these can be accepted as the highest goal of life, none can be regarded as ends in themselves. The most they can do for us is help us reach where the heart wants to reach. So far as our art, our industries, our scientific knowledge, our philosophical speculation help us or contribute to the Supreme Good, the attainment of which is the ideal of man, all are good. But still they have their limitations.

When a person realizes the inherent limitations of this life, how far wealth can take us, how far philosophical knowledge can take us, how far scientific achievement can take us, then he does not remain satisfied with anything temporal here or hereafter. Then he seeks the Eternal and considers the realization of the eternal Truth to be the goal of life. His whole outlook on life changes, so that everything in this world becomes a means to that end. But this attitude does not grow so easily. A person who is generally truthful, sincere, and honest already has his mind purified to a certain extent, and will one day realize the inherent limitations of this life. Then his mind will go beyond the temporal to the search for the eternal. This is what is meant by the purification of the understanding. Clear understanding is necessary; when there is this clear understanding a person turns to the eternal. Then he must have some idea of the eternal Reality, of the Reality behind this universe, of the highest goal of life, of the true nature of man. Next he has to fix his mind on that Reality, and attain the direct experience of that Reality.

SAMADHI OR SUPERCONSCIOUS...

Whatever we know in this world, we know through the mind. Eyes do not reveal these external forms or colours to us, it is the mind behind these eyes. The mind is the common means of the attainment or all knowledge. It is at the back of sense perception, at the back of all inferential knowledge and all rational knowledge. Whatever we know through words, verbal knowledge, comes through the mind. Whenever you know anything, there is a formation in the mind corresponding to that thing. If I tell you of a mountain you will have the knowledge of that mountain because in your mind there will be a mode corresponding, more or less, to the object that I am describing to you. The more your mental mode corresponds to the object, the more you feel you know.

In sense perception we have direct experience of things because our mind comes in contact with the object. Now I am seeing this room—there is a mental mode corresponding to this room. Not only that, in this room there is some contact with the objects I know. So sense perception is capable of revealing to us only what is here and now. Sense perception cannot take us very far. Inferential knowledge, however, has farther range, but it is not immediate, not direct. In inferential knowledge there is the mental mode, but the mental mode does not come in contact with the object known. You go to a house and see the car in the garage, and you think that the owner must be home. This knowledge of the owner being in the house is inferential knowledge, and this mental mode has no contact with the man inside the house. So this knowledge is not always certain. You go into the house and do not find the man. May be his car is out of order, so he could not use it. But when you see the man in the house you have the direct perception, then your mental mode comes in contact with the object of knowledge.

In samadhi there is also a mental mode, and there is also contact of the mental mode with the object known. What is samadhi? We have called it superconscious experience, and it can also be called transcendental experience. This is actually the realization of God, direct experience of the Ultimate Reality. This phenomenal world is held by one eternal, changeless Supreme Being who answers to our conception of perfection in every way. This samadhi or transcendental experience is different from the ecstatic visions many have in religious life. You can hear some strange sound that brings some knowledge to you. You can see certain visions: you may see some light or some figure, which ordinary eyes cannot see. You may even see a form of God. These ecstatic experiences or visions have their value, no doubt, but they are not to be included in the kind of samadhi to be explained in this article.

In this samadhi there is the direct experience of God. God is not actually one of many entities: if you say that God is the greatest of all, then also you fail to describe Him. Why? Because you separate him from all others: God is not apart from anything. He is always described in Vedanta literature as the Supreme Self, the all-pervading reality, the finest of all existences, which penetrates everything, and which is itself not penetrated by anything. That Supreme Reality, all-pervading, interpenetrating everything, is self-shining, of the nature of pure consciousness.

We generally conceive of consciousness as a state of mind, but consciousness in its essential nature is not a state of mind. What we call the conscious state of mind is simply an expression of the essential consciousness, Supreme Spirit, through some modification of the mind. Ultimate Reality is self-existent, self-shining. It is real to Itself, real on its own authority. God is self-existent and self-luminous, real to itself completely, pure awareness. That self-luminous, pure, conscious Supreme Spirit is the essence of each and everything. When a person worships God, sincerely, earnestly, with as much devotion as his heart can command, he can gradually realize that God is not actually far away; God is the reality that makes everything real: all forms and names appear and disappear on the common background of that Reality.

A person, in order to realize God, has to turn inward. The same Supreme Consciousness, all pervading, is manifest within the human individual as the conscious self, the knowing self. This is the central principle in you. Nothing is behind this conscious self. Your mind is objectified, the external world is objectified, the physical body is objectified, the organs are objectified, but beyond all this objectification there is one central, self-luminous principle that is innermost in you. What is innermost in the universe must be innermost in you. What is innermost in an atom must be innermost in every individual. What is innermost in you? Your conscious self. Constant. It shines in waking, in dreaming, in deep sleep. It is distinct from anything experienced. What is experienced is bereft of consciousness. The experiencer alone has consciousness as its very essence. Behind this luminous Self you have to conceive of one effulgent ocean of reality, Supreme Consciousness. Just as behind each and every wave there is a boundless ocean of water, similarly, behind each and every individual consciousness there is the Supreme consciousness. After searching for God here and there and everywhere, a person gradually develops this spiritual sense, that God is the Soul of all souls. God is not one of the many. He is the soul of each and everything.

Where shall I find God? Right within the heart, as the Soul of your soul. To find God, you meditate on the Supreme Consciousness, one infinite ocean of consciousness, pure Spirit. Man is spirit; God is supreme Spirit: there is unity between the two. Try to meditate on your spiritual self and you see a self-effulgent, infinite ocean behind the self. Try to fix your mind on that Reality. The more the mind becomes concentrated, the more the mind takes on the form of that Truth.

In the case of internal perception, the mental mode is always in contact with the object of knowledge. You know what kind of feelings are going on within your heart through your inner perception. Just as you perceive external objects, at the same time you perceive the inner states, and these internal states are directly known.

The mental mode correlates with the mental states, so you directly know that you have pain or pleasure, fear or anger. When we try to meditate on God as the supreme principle, then the mental mode becomes more or less in contact with the Supreme Reality. When the mind becomes purified and pacified completely, tranquil and transparent, it correlates with the Supreme Reality, merges in the Supreme Reality, and that Reality becomes revealed. This transcendental experience also comes through the mind. When the mind becomes tranquil and transparent and correlates with the Reality, then the perception comes. There is some variation in this perception but, on the whole, the mind correlates with the self through deep meditation.

There are two kinds of samadhi. In one state there is some gap between the meditator and the object of meditation. The ego says: "I meditate. I meditate on God." Then this "I," this individual consciousness, becomes united with the Supreme Consciousness, so much so, that there is distinction, but without separation. A person feels his intrinsic relationship with the Supreme Being. This samadhi is called *savikalpa samadhi*. It is the perception of the personal God, but this does not necessarily mean God with form. It means God with attributes. As long as you conceive of God as possessed of all blessed qualities, you personalize Him, whether you think of him with form or not. This is the stage in which the mind becomes united with the Supreme Being and the ego also naturally merges, but still it does not completely drop. A person realizes his deepest relationship with God; but relationship always implies some kind of distinction between the related.

There is a deeper state when this "I" consciousness completely drops, is completely lost, as it were, in the Ocean of Consciousness. This is called *nirvikalpa samadhi*. When this individual consciousness becomes one with the infinite consciousness, there is no distinction between the worshipper and the object of worship, then only one undivided, undiversified, infinite, pure consciousness shines. "I know God, I experience God," this also does not exist.

Sri Ramakrishna lived constantly in samadhi for long periods of time. He said: "What is samadhi? It is the complete merging of the mind in God-Consciousness. The *jnani* (the nondualistic seeker who follows the path of knowledge) experiences *jada samadhi,* in which no trace of 'I' is left. The samadhi attained through the path of *bhakti* is called *'chetana samadhi'*. In this samadhi there remains the consciousness of 'I'—the 'I' of the servant-and-master relationship, of the lover-and-beloved relationship, of the enjoyer-and-food relationship. God is the Master; the devotee is the servant. God is the beloved; the devotee is the lover. God is the food, and the devotee is the enjoyer. "I don't want to be sugar. I want to eat it." He remarks that in nirvikalpa samadhi a person becomes one with the Supreme Reality. But he says that he would rather stay one stage lower and experience the bliss of Brahman than become identified with Brahman.

In both the stages of samadhi, the mind becomes completely tranquil and transparent and is correlated with the Reality. In one case there is "I" consciousness, and in the other, there is no "I" consciousness. This samadhi should not be confused with a state of unconsciousness, some kind of coma or trance, a fainting fit, or even sleep. There is some similarity, it is true, between the transcendental experience and what we call trance or coma or sleep. At the very outset we say that in sleep state you don't know anything of the world, and in samadhi also you don't know anything of the world. But there is a vast difference between the two states.

In the dream state, the mind operates in the subconscious level. In the deep sleep state, the mind goes further down to the bottom and all mental operations cease. You have no fear of any kind, you have no pain or pleasure, no imagination of any kind—it is complete darkness. Your ego becomes merged in that darkness, and all mental operations cease. Something similar to this happens in samadhi. In samadhi the mind, instead of going down into darkness, goes beyond this ego consciousness—it goes above.

The difference between the two states is that, in the deep sleep state, a person enters into the pure darkness of unspecified ignorance. The mind is completely in darkness and ego consciousness does not exist. But when a person goes into transcendental state of samadhi, instead of going into darkness and ignorance, he goes into Light, the Light that is responsible for the manifestation of everything at every moment. The mind enters that Light and a man becomes illumined and all trace of ignorance is removed. He is a transformed person. If an ordinary person, through hard struggle reaches this stage, he becomes an illumined soul. He is free from the bondage of this life completely. There is no death for him : death only exists for those who identify themselves with the body. Those who know they are different from the body, that they are one with the Supreme Reality, beyond birth, growth, decay, and death, hunger and thirst, heat and cold, pain and pleasure, they are ever free.

So these are the two ways the mind can go : you can lose your mind in ego-darkness by letting it gravitate to the lowest depths of your personality, or you can make the effort to raise it to the Light. Every individual is capable of attaining samadhi. It is not the exclusive right of a particular class of people such as the priests or the swamis. Every individual can attain it if he is ready to pay for it. There is a saying, "You get what you pay for." Here also it is true: If you want eternal life you have to pay for eternal life. You can't beguile God and take eternal life like a toy from a child.

You have to reach the superconscious level through effort; you have to go beyond ego through ego; you have to go beyond reason through reason, not by discarding reason; you have to go beyond action through action. Sri

SAMADHI OR SUPERCONSCIOUS... 147

Krishna declares in the *Bhagavad-gita* that you cannot reach the stage of worklessness by simply giving up work. If you want to attain serenity of mind and the ability to live a contemplative life, you have to attain it through the right kind of work. Simply by giving up your duties or by not undertaking duties you cannot reach that state. Through work you go beyond work. If the work is rightly directed, it can lead you beyond work. Similarly, your reason, rightly directed, can lead you beyond its scope. Reason has a limited range, beyond that it is helpless. If you lose your way, you ask a traffic policeman for directions. He will direct you, but will not take you there personally. Reason functions in the same way. A man of God tells you of the nature of God and the world, and of the path to take to realize God, but he cannot take you all the way. You reason on his words and eventually reach the goal, thus using reason to go beyond reason.

Through will you surrender the will. Self-surrender does not mean that you are nothing, a simpleton. There are different kinds of self-surrender in this world. A robber enters your house and says that you have to give all your money to him, otherwise he will kill you. You give him all the money you have : You surrender to him, a compulsory self-surrender. In another case, you understand the worthiness of a great, noble, laudable cause, and you dedicate all you have to that cause : a voluntary self-surrender. Perhaps you find a person who can really guide you, and you submit to his superior knowledge : another kind of self-surrender. Or another man comes and gets you to do certain things by bribing you : another kind of self-surrender. Our will in the foregoing cases is overcome through will.

In the deep sleep state your will simply loses itself. Unsought, sleep comes. If you exercise much volition for sleep you can't get sleep. Your will, in the case of sleep, automatically drops. If you take some kind of intoxicant, your will is stupefied and you lose your consciousness, which is worse than sleep. Sleep gives you some rest, some peace, but through intoxicants you get neither. If you are hypnotized your will is stunned by the blow of another, more powerful will. These are not the methods of attaining the transcendental experience. Only by exercising your will with full reasoning power can you transcend your will and your reason.

There are many psychologists, scientists, and philosophers in this age who confuse the transcendental experience with some kind of unconsciousness. In this world, there is unconsciousness and there is superconsciousness. In the unconscious state you go into the region of darkness, and it does not change your life. You can gain it by intoxicants or through hypnotism by letting your will to be completely stunned or stupefied. But the superconscious state you attain through control of the will. You have to pay a high price for it, by following a certain course and discipline. But one should be careful as there are many fakes and pseudo teachers in the world. Jesus Christ said, "Beware of false prophets."

This superconscious experience is called the fourth kind of experience as distinct from waking, dream and deep sleep. You have to purify your understanding by moral discipline, dutifulness, truth, sincerity, honesty, and then you see this world in all its nakedness. This world is not just a playground. If it is a playground then it is a playground for a very tough school where there are very stern teachers to give you lessons every time you go astray. You must discipline yourself properly, and you will see the right way to live. You follow that method, exercise your will, exercise your reason and go beyond will and reason. Meditate and go beyond the ego-consciousness to the transcendental state. There is the fourth experience, which alone unlocks the spiritual treasure to you forever, which reveals the ultimate reality to you, which is beyond the realm of sense perception and reasoning. When that reality is revealed, you are completely transformed, your innermost longing for eternal life, for absolute peace and blessedness is completely satisfied. All the great mystics of the world declare that such an experience brings supreme satisfaction. They found the goal of all knowledge and the consummation of all joy, the fulfilment of all desires. ❑

9. MEDITATION: ITS PURPOSE AND PRACTICE

The supreme purpose of meditation is to reach the highest goal of life, the direct perception of the Supreme Being, to attain illumination, the light of God-consciousness, which removes all darkness forever, which makes human beings free from all sufferings, bondages, weakness, and imperfection. This goal cannot be reached simply by the study of the scriptures, because scriptural knowledge does not reveal God to us. Similarly, philosophical speculation leads us to indirect knowledge of God; it does not reveal God to us. It is the actual perception of God, seeing God directly, that removes from the heart of humanity the basic ignorance, that primal ignorance from which arises egoism, our deep-seated desire for the temporal, and all our weaknesses. That primal ignorance can be removed only by the light of God-consciousness, and nothing else.

This light of God-consciousness can be attained only through meditation and by no other means.

One of the Upanishads says: "When that Supreme Being, immanent and transcendent, is realized, is seen, then all knots of the heart are cut asunder, all doubts are dispelled, the deposit of past karma is also eliminated, and man attains freedom in every sense." No other spiritual discipline can lead us to this goal. Moral observances and humanitarian deeds can prepare the mind to a great extent for the practice of meditation, as can many modes of worship, but they cannot lead directly to the realization of God. There are different forms of physical, verbal, and mental modes of worship. What is the purpose of these various modes of worship? To bring you close to God, the highest, the best, who is the one ultimate goal of every living being. But no other spiritual practice can bring you as close to God as meditation.

In deep meditation this ego becomes merged in God-consciousness. Through meditation you try to lose yourself completely in God. When you think deeply about a person, you forget yourself, only the consciousness of that person, the beloved one, remains. Similarly, in deep meditation God alone lives in your conscious-

MEDITATION: ITS PURPOSE... 153

ness. The gap between the worshipper and the worshipped is completely filled. When, through deep meditation, the mind becomes completely tranquil and transparent, then the light of the Supreme Spirit shines through the mind, the mind is completely suffused with light, and God-realization comes.

God is present, not far away from us. God is the nearest of all, because He is the very self of the universe, and the innermost Self of each and every one of us. That which is innermost in universe is innermost in every person. Nothing is nearer than God. What we need to do is purify the mind: when the mind is completely purified through the practice of spiritual disciplines, then the light of the Supreme Spirit shines through the mind. Then comes that intuitive perception which is called the direct experience of God. God is always shining there: nothing but the purification of the mind is necessary. So Jesus Christ said: "Blessed are the pure in heart, for they shall see God." Seeing God is the highest blessing; it is the Supreme Beatitude. It is the pure in heart that attain that Supreme Beatitude, therefore, the pure in heart are blessed. Here the highest goal in life is indicated, and the direct means to the attainment of that goal is also declared.

By means other than meditation one can have a vision of God. But God-realization as the innermost Self, as the Reality underlying this universe, as the very basis and being of this manifoldness, cannot come but through meditation. Through prayer you seek the grace of God, and God, out of boundless compassion, may appear to you in a certain form. You can hear the voice of God, you can see God objectively, but that experience is not the ultimate goal of spiritual life, because there is separation. But once you realize God as the very Self, the Supreme Spirit upholding everything, the infinite consciousness that supports and manifests and sustains this universe, then God will ever be manifest in your consciousness, because this individual consciousness will be unified with the Supreme Consciousness.

Realization comes when this individual consciousness communes with the Supreme Consciousness. You reach the Soul of the universe by reaching your own soul. You contact Supreme Spirit through spirit. For each and every kind of experience there is a particular instrument: you perceive the physical form with the physical eyes: you receive the physical

MEDITATION: ITS PURPOSE... 155

sounds through the physical ears: you receive mental ideas through the mind. Similarly, you contact Supreme Spirit through spirit. This individual consciousness is the instrument by which you attain Supreme Consciousness. To realize God as the Supreme Consciousness, you have to meditate on God, lose yourself in God.

Other spiritual practices are necessary to prepare the mind for meditation. A person who wants to practise meditation effectively should be convinced that the direct perception of God is the ideal. Even the slightest awakening of this ideal can be enough for a person to start meditation. A person may be intellectually convinced of this ideal, but still he may not feel longing for this ideal. He may know that this is the goal, that this he should seek, but still, he may not feel the urge to do it. With this kind of awakening there should be some kind of practice to develop that longing, the longing that comes with the purification of the mind.

There are gross and subtle impurities within the mind. As we remove the gross impurities, the subtle appear; then we struggle for the removal of the subtle impurities. We have to observe moral and spiritual disciplines as preparatory steps to meditation. There are many moral courses. Of these, truthfulness, sincerity, and continence are very much emphasized in Hindu spiritual culture. We should observe these moral principles as well as we can. We should also perform our duties of life as faithfully, as efficiently, and as well as we can. We should try to live in a congenial atmosphere and try to guard against adverse influences. If we want to cultivate physical health we must live in a congenial atmosphere; similarly, if we want to cultivate our spiritual life, a congenial atmosphere is necessary. With effort we can avoid many things that are contrary to our spiritual striving.

We should cultivate devotion to God by various methods of worship. As far as our capacities and conditions of life permit, we should engage in spiritual practices, but unless we can develop some devotion to God, we cannot practise meditation on Him. There must be real interest in God. Our mind gets settled upon that in which we are really interested. Whether we seek the absolute, impersonal Being or the personal God, the God possessed of all blessed qualities, in whatever aspect or form we want to realize God, we will have to practise meditation.

There are different modes of worship: physical worship, verbal worship, and mental worship. Of all the different forms of worship, verbal worship is especially emphasized as preparatory to the practice of meditation. That is called *japa*, the repeated utterance of some sacred formula, or holy name of God. This practice of japa is followed by Mohammedan, Christian, and Buddhist devotees as well as Hindu devotees. It is very effective. Japa must go with meditation, because there are many obstructions within us. It is not the external obstacles that prevent the mind from being concentrated on God; it is the inner obstructions. These fluctuations of the mind go on continually. Whether we go into a solitary cave, or whether we live in a crowded city, they are always with us. We can avoid some undesirable persons, or some undesirable surroundings, but the mind will go with us wherever we go, and all our formidable obstructions will arise from the mind. It is not so difficult to get rid of the external obstructions, but it is extremely difficult to get rid of the inner obstructions.

The inner obstructions arise from the deep-seated *samskaras*. Samskaras are the impressions that we have gathered within us from our deeds and our experiences during this life or in past lives. From these impressions, which are like sediment at the bottom of the mind bubbles constantly arise. Thoughts, feelings, and ideas constantly arise, creating fluctuations in the mind. The fluctuations of hatred and love, like and dislike, with regard to every personality, constantly flow within the mind. Our mind also reacts to the external circumstances, favourably and unfavourably, even without any external stimuli. Why? Because our mind is deeply attached to the temporal order. Because of this, our mind has likes and dislikes that are known to us, that we have experienced or dealt with in our past experience, here or anywhere else. If we are completely disinterested in regard to a particular person, we will have neither hatred nor love in regard to that person; we will be indifferent. We do not dislike anything to which we are indifferent. If we dislike a person, that shows that we have some interest there. We cannot be jealous of a person with whom we are in no way concerned.

Because we are concerned in this objective universe with the various sense objects, because we value them someway or other, we have attachments. These attachments create constant fluctuations in the mind, and the mind gets no peace. One way to eliminate these attachments is by creating an interest in the eternal. The more

MEDITATION: ITS PURPOSE... 159

we become interested in eternal values, the more our mind becomes detached from the temporal values. The more we are interested in higher values, the more the mind becomes detached from the lower values. This is the process of human growth.

An interest in the Supreme has to be created by dwelling on the Supreme Being, by worshipping Him, and by repeating his Holy Name. When the mind becomes concentrated on God, when some particular idea is symbolized by a single word upon which one can focus the entire mind, which becomes the very pivot of one's spiritual life, which represents all that divinity means to you, then, if you can hold to such a word or formula, and repeat that, it will work deep into the lower levels of the mind. It will create devotion within you, because it will work against adverse samskaras. These attachments are deeply rooted within us, and are counteracted when we develop devotion to God. Then, and only then, comes dispassion for this world. Therefore, genuine love for God must be developed.

Developing this love for God is not too difficult, because every person is a potential lover of God. What do you love, actually? What do you truly seek? Are you not seeking the permanent in the impermanent? Are you not seeking the perfect in the imperfect? Are you not seeking the infinite in the finite? Can anything finite satisfy you? Can anything imperfect satisfy you? You are wedded to that Supreme Being, because God is the Soul of your soul. There is no rest for you anywhere until you reach That. Love for God is inherent in you; you have only to manifest that love. Cultivation of devotion means only the manifestation of what is already in the heart. If a person is sincere and perseveres in continuing the practice of any of the methods, he can attain devotion to God. When this devotion grows, then you are not as much attached to this world as you were before. Naturally, you can deal with things with a certain measure of dispassion. Without this dispassion it is impossible for you to take an objective view, because you are interested in too many things. The mind has to be detached, more or less, from these transitory forms, which appear so real to us. When the mind is detached, devotion to the Lord grows. The repetition of the sacred word is very important for the development of detachment: Patanjali mentions this as a very efficacious method for the removal of all obstructions. He says that one seed word expressive of the Divine Being is "Om." There are many other seed words. If a person repeats it and tries to understand the meaning, the reality signified by this word; if he contemplates the meaning, and repeats this name, he will perceive the real nature of the Self. He will no longer identify himself only with this psychophysical system.

This psychophysical system is ruled over by a spiritual principle. That principle utilizes the body and the mind as its own instruments. When one becomes aware of the pure spirit, the source of all consciousness, unchanging, witnessing all physical and psychical events, one becomes aware of the Supreme Being that manifests this universe. Just as this microcosm is ruled over by one unchanging, spiritual principle that is responsible for waking, dreaming, and sleeping, and which is aloof from all these experiences, similarly, the entire cosmos is governed by the Supreme Spirit, Pure Consciousness. This invidiual Self is not different from that Supreme Consciousness, essentially. Just as each and every ray belongs to the sun, just as each and every wave belongs to the ocean, similarly, this individual consciousness is one with the Supreme Consciousness that underlies this universe. As a person becomes aware of this truth, obstructions gradually vanish.

What are these obstructions? They appear in the form of distractions: mental lethargy, doubt, fear, restlessness, instability. You try to reach a mental state but you cannot remain there; you slide back. When you repeat the sacred word or formula, the seed word, particularly, all kinds of mental ailments and physical ailments are removed. When these obstructions are removed, the mind gets settled more and more. Meditation is the hardest spiritual practise, because it is the final lesson in spiritual life and discipline.

At present, you may think the goal is very, very high, that you are gaining nothing from this practice of meditation. But this is not the case. You gain with each step you practise. When the mind is purified to a great extent, you will not starve along the way to the goal. You will derive many benefits from the practice. As you become detached from the temporal values, and you have love for God, you will be free from cares and worries to a great extent. There will be calmness, peace, and poise within the mind, and you will have strength within you. The mind is no longer swayed so easily. Your health improves,

MEDITATION: ITS PURPOSE...

your complexion improves, even your voice will improve. You will not feel yourself as just a physical or mental being, subject to birth, growth, decay and death. You will feel yourself as immortal spirit, belonging to the Supreme Lord. What strength you can attain from this consciousness!

You will need some physical posture, called *asana*, when you prepare for and practise meditation. For instance, the Christians observe an asana by kneeling down. The main point is that the body should be at ease and poised, not stiff. The backbone should be straight, and the head and the back should be in one vertical line. Then all the important organs function correctly. The body becomes steady, and you do not get any more resistance from the body; at least, the resistance can be reduced to a minimum. A person can practise *pranayama* (breathing exercises), also, but it is not absolutely necessary. It is very difficult to practise pranayama. Unless a person is very regular in his habits—such as being very moderate in drinking, sleeping, talking, etc.—one cannot successfully practise pranayama. However, if a person can develop some devotion to God, mechanical processes are not very necessary. By worshipping God, by serving the cause of God by different methods, one can develop some devotion. The more you attain natural devotion to God, the less is the necessity for mechanical or physical processes. So these mechanical practices are not indispensible to spiritual growth, although, in some cases, they may help.

In meditation some symbol is very necessary, because we cannot set the mind on the subtle truth, or the abstract reality, unless we get something concrete to hold to. Any object can be a symbol; also a word or a personal form can be a symbol. The sacred word can be used as a visual or audible symbol. When you visualize the word "Om" as radiant, that can serve as the visible symbol. In this case the mental ear and the mental eye are both captured. You can take the resplendent sun, which is the greatest source of light and energy, as the symbol of Divinity. Anything luminous can represent divine consciousness, because God is pure consciousness, pure spirit. A flame that does not flicker, kept in a windless place, can also be visualized as a symbol of divinity. These are impersonal symbols. One can also select some personal symbol. If any great spiritual personality represents divine love to you, or divine wisdom, or divine purity, or divine blessedness, you can also choose that as a subject of meditation. There is a great advantage in choosing a personal form: you establish some relationship between the deity and yourself, the worshipper. There is a reciprocity in that case. You can choose the form of Jesus Christ, or Sri Krishna, or Sri Rama, or Sri Ramakrishna, or you can choose the form of a deity such as Siva, or Kali—whatever represents divinity to you, whatever answers to your conception of the highest ideal.

Any and every kind of imagination will not help you. Meditation is not just wild imagination. There is great scope in meditation, it is true, but every kind of imagination will not help you to reach the goal. That imagination must be based upon man's conception of Reality and must more or less answer to the ideal of perfection. Is there anything in this world, concrete, which represents the best, the highest, to you? That is the question. If a person has any conception of the highest as the Supreme, and if a person can find anything that answers to that conception, he can take it up as a symbol for the practice of meditation. It is not that you are giving full rein to your wild imagination; you have to base this imagination on the highest conception of Reality that you can command.

Practising meditation this way, with the repetition of the holy word or formula, the heart is sanctified. We are often told that if we use some kind of drug we can have an "out-of-body' experience. But such an experience is not what we are looking for. What will it do for you? Suppose you have that kind of experience for a few minutes. You come back from it and where are you? The same place you started from. The questions are: Is your mind sanctified by the experience? Is your mind relieved of these fluctuations that are constantly disturbing you? Is there any power in this world that can relieve you of the play of dark and good forces that is going on within your heart? Go wherever you like and your mind will follow you. If there is a heaven within your mind, that heaven will go with you. If there is a hell within your mind, that hell will go with you. Remember this! You may try to escape from undesirable persons, undesirable environments, but they will follow you wherever you go. Take up a holy word, or a holy symbol, and continue your spiritual practices.

The great seers have dominated human consciousness for centuries. Although there have been many philosophers, scientists, and poets in this world, did they have such a great following

MEDITATION: ITS PURPOSE...

as has Jesus Christ, Buddha, Sri Krishna, or Sri Ramakrishna? The reason these great spiritual leaders have such a following is because there is a difference in the intrinsic value of their knowledge and the intrinsic value of secular knowledge. In meditation on these great souls there is no fear of being lost in a kind of wild imagination. There is no fear you will become egocentric, because you gain with every step of spiritual practice.

The purpose of meditation is to relieve you of your ego-centeredness and make you God-centered. You may sit quietly and ponder over your problems and live an isolated life, or you may move about in the world, ostensibly doing good to the world. Still, you are trying to exploit the world in every way. You want to secure more wealth, name, fame, and position for yourself. Watch and see how much ego-centeredness there is. If there is any method of curing one of ego-centredness, it is God-centredness. You can become God-centred by practising any one of the modes of worship. The more you are interested in God, the more you know your spiritual relationship with the Divine Being, the more you will find others also spiritually related to God, and spiritually related to you.

The main difficulty is finding the spiritual relationship with others. Only the realization of common interests will not help us very much. Common economic interest, common political interest, common social interest cannot go very far. With that interest there will be some kind of contrary interest. But there should be a sense of spiritual relationship, because it is common to all. Spirit is deeper than racial distinction, deeper than the distinction of merit. Spiritual relationship is the deepest of all. It transcends all differences of culture and of race. When you become conscious of that spiritual relationship, you find a bond with all humanity. That deeper spiritual relationship comes with the awareness of the spiritual nature of a person, and also with the awareness of one's spiritual relationship with the Supreme Being. The more a person becomes God-centred, the greater will be his love for humanity.

A person has to cultivate devotion to God by the various methods given for the practice of meditation, and practise meditation every day. We do not lose anything, rather, we gain—even in our secular interests. How much time we lose in making mistakes, how much energy we lose. There will be fewer mistakes, and less frittering away of energy. When the mind is purified, there is true insight within us, so there cannot be any difficulty which we cannot solve. By the practice of meditation we gain, not only spiritually, but also in a worldly way. Success is sure; there cannot be any failure in this. If we walk one step towards the right goal it is a definite gain. But if we walk thousands of steps toward the wrong goal, we will have to retrace our steps. Know what is the right goal of life and the right path to take; pursue the course and gain with each step you take.

It is through the practice of meditation that the mind actually realizes God. One of the Upanishads states: "That Supreme Being cannot be seen with the eyes, cannot be expressed with words, cannot be touched with the hands, none of these organs of action or the organs of perception, or the mind, can comprehend That." When the understanding is purified, when you realize the true purpose of life, when you have right understanding, then your thinking, your feeling, your willpower will be right. A person must have the right attitude towards the world and life. When this understanding is purified, then the mind becomes purified. When the mind is purified, then a person can effectively practise meditation. Through the practice of deep meditation, when the mind becomes tranquil and transparent, intuitive perception develops. Then one realizes the Supreme Being, the light of God-consciousness, the light that counteracts the primal ignorance from which proceed all weakness, all imperfection, all bondage and suffering. The only cure from this primal ignorance is the practice of meditation. Jesus Christ has stated: "The kingdom of God is within you." "Blessed are the pure in heart for they shall see God." ❑

10. PSYCHIATRY AND VEDANTA

While the treatment of mental illness is the primary role of psychiatry, it is a subsidiary function for Vedanta. Psychiatry, a special branch of medical science, is concerned particularly with ailing persons; the religion and philosophy of Vedanta (like other systems of thought and culture in general) deals especially with normal human beings. Its primary function is to develop humans intellectually, morally, and spiritually, and to prevent their deterioration. Normal individuals, too, have mental troubles such as disquiet and distractions and emotional disturbances. When occasion arises, Vedantic teachers undertake therapeutic work. The knowledge of the human mind that Vedanta provides is adequate for the purpose.

The scope of Vedantic therapy is, however, limited in a sense. Mental ailments due solely or primarily to physical causes, such as the diseases of the nervous system and the bodily organs, Vedantic teachers leave to the care of psychiatrists and medical doctors. They usually restrict themselves to psychogenic cases, the treatment of which must be, in their view, at the psychological level. According to certain statistical accounts, eighty percent of the medical cases in America are psychogenic. Because the actual cause of the trouble is in the mind, it often cannot be reached by purely physical treatment. The cause has to be determined by psychological analysis, which need not be the same as psychoanalysis, probing in the lowest depths of the mind. Vedantic psychotherapy aims to cure mental and functional disorders due to fear, anxiety, frustration, internal conflict, guilt, suppressed desire, and so forth, by rectifying the patient's inner attitude towards the object concerned—things, beings, or events, as the case may be—and thereby transforming his reactions to them. He is taught how to adapt himself to the varying conditions of life, since the stress due to social maladjustment contributes to neurosis and to psychosis as well. But to effect a permanent cure Vedanta recommends changing one's outlook on life, because the root cause of mental ailment is a wrong view of life. All the while the patient is to be treated with due consideration of his capacities; he who feels for the patient heals his heart.

As long as one looks upon pleasures and possessions as the primary objectives of life, one cannot be free from emotional involvement. One who is attached to his riches must have the fear of losing them and the consequent cares and worries. He will be envious of those who have more than he has, contemptuous of those who have not enough, and proud of what he has. Greed invariably takes hold of him. Sense desires are insatiable, while the means of their fulfilment are inadequate. The objects of desire, transitory as they are, cannot be easily acquired. The body and the organs, the instruments of sense enjoyment, give way before the mind is satisfied. The baneful effects of modern living—constant tension, discontent, competition, conflict—are inevitable, inasmuch as one and all clamour for maximum power and prosperity as the very goal of life. Vedanta does not condemn the search for pleasures and possessions, but urges the seekers not to look upon them as ends in themselves. This draws man's attention from the lower to the higher ideals until he finds the highest. When the mind turns to the higher values it invariably becomes detached from the lower. This is the way to outgrow sense desires. That Vedanta recommends. Vedanta condemns their suppression and repression no less than over-indulgence. Detachment does not, however, mean indifference. Human desires and emotions are not wrong in themselves, otherwise they could not be sublimated. They have to be given higher and higher directions until they turn to God, the Highest. Self-control implies uplifting oneself.

Vedanta agrees with psychiatry on the point that man should be viewed as an integrated whole. But the difference is this, psychiatry conceives man as a psychological organism, of which the physical system is the prime factor, and ignores his spiritual self. Vedanta recognizes, as religions generally do, three distinct factors in human personality—body, mind and spirit, among which the spiritual self is the basic unifying principle. So the real man is not the unity of the three factors, but the central principle of consciousness that integrates the body and the mind and functions as the knower and as the doer in association with them.

The mind has the capacity to transmit consciousness that belongs to the knowing Self. In addition, though distinct, the body and the mind are closely associated and influence each other. A man's problems cannot be solved effectively unless he has a correct view of himself. The truer the view, the better is the life. Not only should he be acquainted with his present status or stage of development but also with his fundamental nature. Is man basically a physical, a psychophysical, or a spiritual being? On his answer to these questions depend his ideal and plan of living—the key to the integration of personality. Until he knows the true meaning of life no inner stability is possible. None can be at peace with himself unless he can find a satisfactory answer to the question, "What do I live for?" It is the recognition of the spiritual Self, ever shining, birthless, growthless, decayless, deathless, that gives a man a sense of security amidst all the uncertainties of life, removes his fears, awakens his self-faith—the key to his development—and makes him the master of himself. At the same time he recognizes the spiritual Self of others and treats them with love and respect. The root cause of man's troubles is the ignorance of the true nature of the Self.

One of the Upanishads gives a graphic picture of man's journey to the ultimate Goal with self-mastery:

> Know the (spiritual) Self to be the master of the chariot, and the body, the chariot. Know right understanding to be the charioteer and the mind (volitional) the reins. The senses are said to be the horses and the objects, the roads. The wise call the Self associated with the body, the senses, and the mind the experiencer. ... A man who has right understanding of his charioteer and holds the reins of the mind firmly reaches the end of the road; and that is the supreme position of the omnipresent, all transcendent Being (Katha I, iii.3)

Man's self-fulfilment is not in physical, intellectual, aesthetic, or moral well-being, but in spiritual enlightenment. Because it is conducive to the highest good, spiritual life is of supreme importance in Vedantic thought and culture. Next to this is man's moral life. Psychiatry has paid little attention to either of these. Moral goodness is a prerequisite for spiritual awakening. Not only that, it sustains man's intellectual, aesthetic, physical and social well-being. Who can expect to maintain good health unless he lives with moderation and self-restraint? Virtue brightens intellect and develops the power of discrimination between the pleasant and the beneficial, the apparent and the real, the ephemeral and the eternal. It counteracts emotional imbalance. Humility overcomes pride; charity overcomes unkindness; loving sympathy overcomes anger and hate. When unsupported by moral judgment, aesthetic sensuousness turns into sensuality. Without fair dealings with our fellow-beings no sound interpersonal relationship is possible. Tension and hostility in collective life, potent causes of nervous breakdown and mental disorder, are inevitable.

Besides the conscious and the subconscious states on which man usually dwells, Vedanta recognizes the superconscious state, which none but the specially qualified can reach. In the conscious, the waking state, a person experiences external objects and internal facts as well. But he cannot see the entire mind. The part of the mind that is open to the waking ego is the conscious level; below this is the subconscious; and beyond this is the superconscious. In dream and deep sleep the experiencer dwells on the subconscious level. Normally, every individual experiences three different states—waking, dream, and deep sleep—every day. They do not bring about radical change in his vision of life and the world. It is the superconscious experience that reveals the truth regarding the Self and the universe and its Ruler, removes his bondage forever and reinstates him to his native purity, freedom, and blissfulness. The basic urge in man is the urge for perfection. This he attains by Self-realization, which is the same as the realization of God, the Soul of all souls.

Vedanta highly values the conscious or the waking state. It is then and then only that man's reason and volition function. It is by the exercise of will backed by reason, that man has to regulate his emotions and actions to achieve anything worthwhile. There is no progress in the subconscious level and no moral judgement is possible there. In dreaming and in drunkenness all mental operations are involuntary; only emotions and instincts prevail. What can man achieve then? It is his volitional action that separates the human level from the subhuman and enables him to rise above the sense plane: the performance of volitional action is the special privilege of human life. In lower levels instinct prevails. Any volitional operation, physical or mental, is karma. Right or wrong, high or low, this leaves a corresponding impression on the mind. By our deliberate actions and experiences we are constantly storing in the mind various impressions or samskaras. Our ideas and emotions, tendencies and desires, capabilities and memories, are derived from them. When manifest in the conscious mind, they control behaviour. The impressions also dwell within as retributive moral forces that fructify in due course here or here-after and create favourable or unfavourable situations. Being close to the surface these influence the conscious mind and behaviour more or less. They account for what some psychologists like to call "the unconscious mental processes" in preference to "the unconscious". But most of the unmanifest impressions lie dormant in the bottom of the mind. They affect neither the conscious mind nor behaviour as long as they remain dormant. They may become manifest in the conscious level in due course. Thus in the Vedantic view, the subsoil of the mind is the repository of both good and evil elements; it is not dreadful or abominable as the unconscious described by Freud. It cannot be said that only suppressed urges dwell there. Whatever thought, emotions, and propensities prevail in the conscious mind naturally gravitate to the subconscious level. Necessarily, the endogenous cause of mental ailments has to be traced there.

When the departing spirit leaves the physical body, it retains the mind with all its contents in seed form. In due course the spirit is reborn with them, unless it has attained liberation. It is the unredeemed souls that become reincarnate. Because the mind and the body are distinct, the characteristics of the one cannot inhere in the other. However, psychiatry posits hereditary transmission to account for the endogenous cause of mental illness. But in the Vedantic view this is not possible unless we acknowledge that some parts of the parents' mind enter into the gene at conception. In that case it is to be admitted that each time a child is born the parents must lose portions of their minds. But this is not so. It is also a fact that children do not necessarily inherit the parents' intellectual, aesthetic, moral or spiritual nature. Wicked children are born of saintly parents, sane children of insane parents. A congenital defect, mental or physical, is not necessarily hereditary.

The direct knowledge of the human mind is possible only by introspection. The study of behaviour is an indirect approach. Vedanta does not depend on the latter as much as on the former. Generally speaking, human behaviour is not instinctive as is animal behaviour. Man's judgment intervenes between his thoughts and emotions and their expression. For example, a person may be aware of a fact, still he may deny it and pretend ignorance. He may not eat the food offered to him even though he may like it. With no happiness within, one may appear to be happy. With no love within, one can make a show of love. Experimental psychology, on which psychiatry mainly depends, being based primarily on the observation of external behaviour, cannot be expected to provide adequate knowledge of the human mind.

The main difference between psychiatry and Vedanta is in their conceptions of human personality. I have tried to indicate that in the treatment of mental illness physical therapy and mental therapy have their respective places. But both have to be supplemented with a comprehensive and consistent view of human personality and the values of life. Man lives on different levels of life. He is meant for the highest. Until he finds a way to it he cannot have peace of mind. ❏